A GUIDE BOOK
OF
ENGLISH COINS

Nineteenth
and
Twentieth Centuries

To produce the outstanding coinage described in this book, the Royal Mint has made many experimental tests on alloys and production methods with die trial pieces like the rarely seen example shown here.

A GUIDE BOOK

of

ENGLISH COINS

NINETEENTH AND TWENTIETH CENTURIES

Eighth Edition

By

KENNETH E. BRESSETT

A Complete, Illustrated Valuation
Catalogue of Modern English Coins
with Official Reports of Coinage
Figures for Each Year and His-
torical Notes About Each Issue.

 Whitman Coin Products

WESTERN PUBLISHING COMPANY, INC.

RACINE, WISCONSIN 53404

No. 9060 Printed in U.S.A.

ISBN: 0-307-09060-4

FOREWORD

Many people have helped in the compilation of this catalogue. Thomas Mowery produced the premier edition which pointed the way to what collectors needed for a handy, useful coverage of the subject.

Sincere thanks are due to Mr. D. F. Starck of the Royal Mint for his part in supplying accurate listings of early mint reports; to Mr. Robert C. Willey for making his collection available for photography and to Mr. Alfred E. Petrie for allowing me to study and photograph coins in the Canadian National Archives. Messrs. William Clark and Sawyer McA. Mosser also helped by supplying photographs of coins in the collection of the American Numismatic Society.

Collectors of English coins should find this catalogue a convenient source of easy-to-find information and an accurate guide to present day valuations of their coins. The casual inquirer, too, will find no difficulty in locating coins in this book and finding out all he wants to know about them.

In keeping with other **WHITMAN** coin catalogues, each type of coin is illustrated and discussed prior to the listings covering dates and values. Coins are grouped according to denomination, from the smallest to the largest.

To further your interest in the field of collecting English coins, the following publications are recommended as excellent sources of information and current values:

The Numismatic Circular
Spink & Son Ltd.
5-7 King Street
St. James's
London, S.W.1, England

B. A. Seaby, Ltd.
Audley House
11 Margaret Street
Oxford Circus
London, WIN 8AT, England

Coins and Medals
Link House
Dingwall Avenue
Croydon, CR9 2TA, England

World Coins
P. O. Box 150
Sidney, Ohio   45365

World Coin News
Iola, Wisconsin   54945

PANEL OF CONTRIBUTORS TO THE EIGHTH EDITION

Q. David Bowers
James Clune
Peter Gaspar
James Haxby
John Hunter
F. J. Jeffery
Christopher Josset
Richard Lobel
Reginald Lubbock

Raymond Merena
Rosco T. Parmley
P. Alan Rayner
Neil Shafer
Philip Starr
Richard Trowbridge
Holland Wallace
James W. Wells

INTRODUCTION

This catalogue covers the history and coinage of Great Britain from the last few years of the eighteenth century up to the present date. It was during this period, starting in 1797, that the first of the modern English coins began to appear. The modernization was largely due to the efforts of Matthew Boulton, who designed new equipment and minting techniques.

During the years 1810-1812 the present Royal Mint was built and powerful machinery was erected by Boulton and Watt. In 1816 a complete new issue of coinage was started. Half crowns, shillings and sixpence were struck during that year. The silver issue was reduced in size and weight to sixty-six shillings instead of sixty-two to the troy pound.

The improvement in coinage was an outgrowth of Britain's rise as a world power in the nineteenth century. The prevalent bank tokens, private tokens, counterstamped Spanish dollars and even counterfeit coppers, could not be used in world trade. With a new coinage it became possible to introduce the British monetary system to her thriving colonies, which had previously used other systems. To make this more palatable certain special British denominations were coined to bridge the new and old colonial systems. Except by denomination these special issues were indistinguishable from the regular British coins.

The groat (4 pence silver, 1838-56, 1888), was a substitute for the old ¼ guilder used in British Guiana. The ¼ farthing (1839-53) and ½ farthing (1839-56) were coined as rough equivalents of ½ and 1 doit and ½ and 1 Indian pie. The 1½ pence (1838-62) was roughly equal to the Indian anna, and to the Spanish-American ¼ real used in Jamaica. The ⅓ farthing (1844-1913) substituted for Malta's 1 grano. Although made for colonial use, these fractional coins rightfully belong in a British type set and have been included in this catalogue.

The first coins ever used in England were probably those that were coined in Gaul in the early part of the second century B.C. These coins were close imitations of gold coins issued by Philip of Macedon and were called *philippi*. In Gaul these coins became more and more crude as they were imitated by each generation, and by the time they reached Great Britain and were still further imitated, they had degenerated to simply surrealistic patterns which hardly resembled the originals.

Roman coinage was introduced to the country at the time of the conquest by Julius Caesar and first minted in Britain by Carausius (287-293 A.D.), who reigned in Britain and a small part of Gaul. Mints were established at London and Colchester and money was coined on the Roman standard until 388 A.D.

The earliest of the true English coins are known as *sceattas*. They are small, thick pieces of many varieties and types. In most cases they are without the name of any king or any legend whatsoever. The few inscriptions which do appear on these coins indicate that they were struck about 650 A.D.

Toward the end of the eighth century, under the influence of a change which had taken place in the coinage of France, the small, thick *sceat* was replaced by a thinner, but much broader piece which was known as a *penny*. It was first coined during the reign of Offa, King of Mercia 757-795 A.D. The corresponding coins of France were based on a standard devised by Charlemagne, who used the basic unit of a pound of solid silver. This corresponded to the Roman *aes grave,* which was a large bronze coin weighing one Roman pound. Charlemagne's silver coins were called *deniers* (from the Latin *denarius*). King Offa divided the pound into 240 parts and issued silver pennies with a value of 1/240 of a pound.

It is interesting to note that the reverse side of most of these early pennies was decorated with a cross which served a dual purpose as a religious symbol and as a convenient guide for dividing the coins into two parts for half pennies or four parts for quarter pennies, which were called *farthings* from the Anglo-Saxon word *feurthing* meaning ¼.

During the reign of Edward III, new coins were added to the silver pennies originated by King Offa. Edward III established a complete coinage system containing gold and silver coins of several denominations. The first shillings were issued about 100 years later by Henry VII (1485-1509). The shilling was worth 12 pence or 1/20 of a pound. The name shilling was derived from the Anglo-Saxon word *scilling,* meaning "to divide."

The present-day symbol for the pound, £, stands for the Roman word *libra,* meaning pound. The small s, which designates the shilling, originally stood for *solidus,* a Roman coin that circulated in England during the occupation.

Thus the British monetary units, as they evolved through the centuries, were not a decimal system but rather cumbersome fractions of the Roman libra. In 1971 an entirely new system based on decimal divisions of the current English pound became standardized, and sterling coins were withdrawn from circulation.

Modern gold coins are the half pound (or half sovereign, equivalent to 10 shillings), one pound, two pounds and five pounds. The gold guinea, last minted in 1813, was equivalent to 21 shillings. Bullion gold coins, in the form of sovereigns, are still minted but these are not intended for circulation within the monetary system.

The shilling was commonly known as a "bob"; the sixpence occasionally called a "tanner" and the pound a "quid." A table of sterling coin equivalents is as follows:

2 Farthings = 1 Halfpenny	2 Shillings = 1 Florin
2 Halfpennies = 1 Penny (1 d)	2½ Shillings = 1 Half Crown
3 Pennies = 1 Threepence	5 Shillings = 1 Crown
6 Pennies = 1 Sixpence	20 Shillings = 1 Pound (£)
12 Pennies = 1 Shilling	21 Shillings = 1 Guinea

Under the decimal system the pound is now divided into 100 new pence. The symbol £ has been retained as the recognized abbreviation for the pound, while its fractional parts, called new pence, are abbreviated with the letter p.

SOVEREIGNS OF GREAT BRITAIN

STUART LINE

James I — (1603-1625)
Charles I — (1625-1649)
Commonwealth and
  Protectorate — (1649-1659)
Charles II — (1660-1685)
James II — (1685-1688)

HOUSE OF ORANGE

William III and
  Mary II — (1689-1694)
William III, alone — (1694-1702)

STUART LINE

Anne — (1702-1714)

HOUSE OF HANOVER

George I — (1714-1727)
George II — (1727-1760)
George III — (1760-1820)
George IV — (1820-1830)
William IV — (1830-1837)
Victoria — (1837-1901)

SAXE-COBURG LINE

Edward VII — (1901-1910)

HOUSE OF WINDSOR

George V — (1910-1936)
Edward VIII — (1936)
George VI — (1936-1952)
Elizabeth II — (1952-   )

CONVERSION TABLES

£ N.P.	U.S. $ ¢	£ N.P.	U.S. $ ¢
£0·01	$ .02	£3·00	$6.60
0·02	.04	3·50	7.70
0·03	.07	4·00	8.80
0·04	.09	4·50	9.90
0·05	.11	5·00	11.00
0·06	.13	5·50	12.10
0·07	.15	6·00	13.20
0·08	.18	6·50	14.30
0·09	.20	7·00	15.40
0·10	.22	7·50	16.50
0·15	.33	8·00	17.60
0·20	.44	8·50	18.70
0·25	.55	9·00	19.80
0·30	.66	10·00	22.00
0·35	.77	12·00	26.40
0·40	.88	14·00	30.80
0·50	1.10	15·00	33.00
0·60	1.32	18·00	39.60
0·70	1.54	20·00	44.00
0·80	1.76	25·00	55.00
0·85	1.87	30·00	66.00
0·90	1.98	40·00	88.00
0·95	2.09	50·00	110.00
1·00	2.20	60·00	132.00
1·25	2.75	70·00	154.00
1·50	3.30	80·00	176.00
2·00	4.40	90·00	198.00
2·50	5.50	100·00	220.00

APPROXIMATE BRITISH EQUIVALENTS OF U.S. DOLLARS

U.S. $ ¢	£ N.P.	U.S. $ ¢	£ N.P.
$ .05	£0·02	$4.00	£1·82
.10	0·05	5.00	2·27
.20	0·09	10.00	4·55
.25	0·11	15.00	6·82
.50	0·23	20.00	9·09
.75	0·34	25.00	11·36
1.00	0·45	50.00	22·73
2.00	0·91	75.00	34·09
3.00	1·36	100.00	45·46

EXPLANATION OF CONDITIONS OF COINS AND
OTHER NUMISMATIC TERMS USED IN THIS BOOK

PROOF — On certain occasions the mint is authorized to strike special coins known as "proofs." In preparing these coins, the dies and metal blanks are highly polished and the coins are struck with great pressure and care. Proof coins can be distinguished by their sharpness of detail and extremely brilliant, mirror-like surface. Specimen sets of proof coins were usually issued for presentation purposes on the occasion of the introduction of a new type of coinage and for the coronation of a new monarch. These coins are not intended for circulation and often have an edge device that is different from the regular coins.

Prior to 1887, proof coins were privately sold by mint officials. The proof sets of 1902 all have a dull, "matte," surface produced by the use of chemicals in the finishing process which removes the brilliant surface and leaves the coins with a frosted iridescent finish. The term "proof" describes the method of manufacture of a coin and not its condition. Occasionally, proof coins show signs of wear or abuse.

The term "Fleur-de-coin" (FDC) is often used to designate a coin in perfect flawless mint state — either uncirculated or proof.

UNCIRCULATED — The term uncirculated is usually abbreviated, Unc. It is used to describe a coin that has never been used as money and is still in the same new condition as the day it was minted. A coin with even the slightest sign of wear cannot qualify for this condition.

Uncirculated coins frequently lose their original mint brilliance or become tarnished with age, which decreases their value. Older copper or bronze coins with full mint lustre (bright reddish or gold color) are valued higher than ordinary uncirculated coins.

Farthings minted from 1897 to 1918 have a special blackened finish to distinguish them from gold coins. Certain pennies coined during the war years were also darkened at the mint to save them from being hoarded. These coins, although in uncirculated condition, do not have the usual brilliant surface.

EXTREMELY FINE (Ex. Fine) — Once a coin has received slight wear from handling or contact with other coins, it is no longer uncirculated and is called "extremely fine" or occasionally, "about uncirculated." A coin in this condition has the appearance of being in perfect condition with the exception of very minor flaws or friction spots.

VERY FINE (V. Fine)—A coin in "very fine" condition shows signs of having been in circulation and the highest points on the coin are slightly flattened from wear. A "very fine" coin must have all of the fine line details of the design still showing and can have no disfiguring nicks or scratches.

FINE — Coins in "fine" condition have been worn from considerable use in circulation. Many parts of the coin, including the outer raised rim, will be rounded or flattened from wear. Minor nicks and blemishes are to be expected.

The overall appearance, however, is still pleasing and all details still show clearly.

GOOD — Common coins are not often collected in "good" condition. Rare or valuable coins in this condition are sometimes saved when no others are available. A "good" coin is one that is so worn that most of the details are flat and numerous nicks and scratches may be present. All of the principal design and lettering must be discernible.

COINAGE FIGURES — The figures listed in this book under "quantity minted" indicate the number of coins minted each year, as stated in the official reports from the Royal Mint. These quantities refer to the number of pieces coined in a given year but do not necessarily mean that the coins bear that particular date. The proper corrections have been made (and noted) when discrepancies such as this are known. The quantity of coins minted originally does not necessarily relate to the present day rarity of a coin.

MINT MARKS — Nearly all British coins have been minted at the Royal Mint in London, or since decimalization at the new mint at Llantrisant. These coins do not bear any special marking to indicate where they were coined. Several branch mints have been established in various cities over the years in order to produce sufficient quantities of coins for the United Kingdom. All branch mint coins have a special mark to indicate their place of origin. The mint marks found on British coins are as follows:

- C — Ottawa, Canada
- H — Ralph Heaton and Sons, The Mint, Birmingham, Ltd.
- I — Bombay, India
- KN — Kings Norton Metal Co., Birmingham
- M — Melbourne, Australia
- P — Perth, Australia
- SA — Pretoria, South Africa
- SOHO — Soho Mint, Birmingham
- S — Sydney, Australia

PICTURES — The illustrations in this book are photographs of actual coins. All of these are shown in true size.

PRICES — Valuations in this catalogue are an average of the current prices that collectors pay for each coin as ascertained from dealers' stocks, price lists, sales catalogues and recent auction sales. These prices are not an offer to buy or sell coins and neither the author nor publisher deals in coins.

DESCRIPTIONS — The OBVERSE of a British coin is the side on which the monarch's head appears. The opposite side is called the REVERSE. The LEGEND is the inscription, which is usually in Latin. A cut blank of metal, prepared for coinage, is known as a PLANCHET or FLAN. Each different design is referred to as a TYPE. A minor refinement or change in a TYPE is known as a VARIETY.

BRITISH COLONIAL COINS

Quarter-, third- and half-farthings were struck for use in some of the colonies that used the other English coins. They are generally included in collections of this series. The half-farthings were made current in England in 1842 but never circulated extensively.

COPPER QUARTER-FARTHINGS

This fractional farthing was coined solely for use in Ceylon. The obverse shows the head of the queen and was struck from dies of the Maundy two-pence. This denomination was roughly the equivalent of $\frac{1}{2}$ doit and $\frac{1}{2}$ Indian pie. The regular issue is struck in copper. A few proof specimens were struck in bronze. Dies by William Wyon.

Diameter: 13.50mm; weight: 1.18 grams; composition: copper; edge: plain.

  Victoria 1837-1901

Perfect bright red uncirculated coins command higher prices.

Date	Quantity Minted	Good	Fine	V. Fine	Ex. Fine	Unc.	Proof
1839 3,840,000		$5.00	$8.00	$15.00	$30.00	$50.00	——
1851 .... ⎱		5.00	9.00	17.00	40.00	60.00	——
1852 .... ⎬ 2,215,680		4.00	6.00	12.00	25.00	45.00	$200.00
1853 .... ⎰		5.00	9.00	20.00	50.00	70.00	200.00
1868 Proof only							400.00

COPPER THIRD-FARTHINGS

These coins were made for use in Malta and were the first pieces issued specially for the island after it became a British possession. The regular English farthing was already circulating there as three Maltese grains and the new coin was made of similar design and exactly one-third the weight, to pass as one grain. Dies by William Wyon. A total of 3,951,520 pieces dated 1827 and 1835 was coined.

Diameter: 16.25mm; weight: 1.58 grams; composition: copper; edge: plain.

  George IV 1820-1830

1827	2.00	4.00	10.00	20.00	30.00	80.00

  William IV 1830-1837

1835	1.75	3.50	9.00	17.50	25.00	80.00

[11]

British Colonial Coins

Victoria 1837-1901

Date	Quantity Minted	Good	Fine	V. F.	Ex. F.	Unc.	Proof
1844 REG rev.	}1,301,040	$5.00	$12.00	$20.00	$40.00	$80.00	
1844 RE rev.		10.00	30.00	70.00	150.00	250.00	

BRONZE THIRD-FARTHINGS

Third-farthings issued for use in Malta in 1866 and later are struck in bronze. The head of Victoria is from dies by L. C. Wyon after a model by W. Theed. Several minor die varieties exist in the number of leaves and acorns in the wreath.

Diameter: 15.50mm; weight: 0.95 grams; composition: .950 copper, .040 tin, .010 zinc; edge: plain.

Victoria 1837-1901

Date	Quantity	Good	Fine	V.F.	Ex.F.	Unc.	Proof
1866	576,000	1.50	3.00	6.00	10.00	25.00	$100.00
1868	144,000	1.50	3.00	6.00	10.00	25.00	150.00
1876	162,000	1.75	3.50	7.00	12.00	30.00	
1878	288,000	1.50	3.00	6.00	10.00	25.00	
1881	144,000	1.75	3.50	7.00	12.00	30.00	130.00
1884	144,000	1.50	3.00	6.00	10.00	25.00	
1885	288,000	1.50	3.00	6.00	10.00	25.00	

Edward VII 1901-1910

Date	Quantity	Good	Fine	V.F.	Ex.F.	Unc.
1902	288,000	1.00	1.25	1.75	3.50	9.00

George V 1910-1936

Date	Quantity	Good	Fine	V.F.	Ex.F.	Unc.
1913	288,000	1.00	1.50	2.00	4.00	10.00

COPPER HALF-FARTHINGS

The copper half-farthing was originally made for use in Ceylon. It was made current for use in the United Kingdom by a proclamation in 1842 and remained so until demonetized along with all copper coinage in 1869.

Diameter: 17.50mm; weight: 2.37 grams; composition: copper; edge: plain.

George IV 1820-1830

Two different reverse varieties occur: Variety I with trident prongs slightly above the base of the lettering and Variety II with trident touching the base of the letters.

Perfect bright red uncirculated coins command higher prices.

Date	Quantity Minted	Good	Fine	V. F.	Ex. F.	Unc.	Proof
1828 var. I....	} 7,680,000	$4.50	$10.00	$20.00	$40.00	$70.00	$150.00
1828 var. II...		5.00	12.00	25.00	50.00	90.00	
1830 var. I....	} 8,776,320	4.50	10.00	22.50	45.00	80.00	
1830 var. II...		5.00	12.00	27.50	60.00	100.00	175.00

William IV 1830-1837

1837.........1,935,360		7.00	15.00	30.00	80.00	120.00	

Victoria 1837-1901

Variety I 1839   Variety II 1842-1868

When this denomination was declared a current coin in 1842, the reverse was changed to show a rose, thistle and shamrock to make it more uniform with the three higher denominations. Proof specimens struck in bronze or bronzed copper are occasionally seen. On these the obverse and reverse are rotated 180°. Dies were by William Wyon.

Date	Good	Fine	V. F.	Ex. F.	Unc.	Proof
1839.........2,042,880	1.75	4.00	9.00	22.00	32.00	100.00
1842.................	1.50	3.00	8.00	18.00	27.50	
1843.........3,440,640	.50	1.00	2.00	3.00	7.00	
1844.........	.50	1.00	1.50	2.50	6.00	
1844 N over E* } 6,451,200	2.00	5.00	15.00	30.00	50.00	
1847.........3,010,560	1.00	2.50	6.00	13.00	25.00	
1851.................	1.75	4.00	9.00	20.00	27.50	
1852...........989,184	1.75	4.00	9.00	20.00	27.50	
1853...........955,224	2.00	5.00	10.00	27.50	50.00	75.00
1854...........677,376	2.00	7.00	15.00	30.00	55.00	
1856 lg. date.... } 913,920	Rare					
1856 sm. date...	2.00	7.00	16.00	35.00	60.00	
1868 Proof only						200.00

*This variety has the E in REGINA overpunched with an N.

British Colonial Coins

SILVER THREE-HALFPENCES

These coins were never issued for circulation in England. They were struck for use in Ceylon, British Guiana, and the British West Indies, which used the ordinary British currency. They were a rough equivalent to the Indian anna and to the Spanish-American ¼ real used in Jamaica and are similar to the silver Maundy coins except for the crowned 1½ on reverse. All of these coins have the obverse and reverse rotated 180°, except the 1870 which is not rotated.

Diameter: 12.40mm; weight: 0.71 grams; composition: .925 silver, .075 copper; edge: plain.

William IV 1830-1837

Date	Quantity Minted	Good	Fine	V. F.	Ex. F.	Unc.	Proof
1834	800,448	$1.00	$2.00	$4.25	$9.00	$20.00	
1835 5 over 4	633,600	3.00	10.00	20.00	40.00	75.00	
1835		1.00	2.00	4.50	10.00	20.00	
1836	158,400	1.00	2.00	4.50	10.00	20.00	
1837	30,624	2.50	7.00	16.00	35.00	60.00	

Victoria 1837-1901

1843, 43 over 34

Date	Quantity Minted	Good	Fine	V. F.	Ex. F.	Unc.	Proof
1838	538,560	1.00	2.25	5.00	10.00	20.00	
1839	760,320	1.00	2.00	4.25	9.00	18.00	
1840	95,040	1.50	5.00	10.00	22.00	35.00	
1841	158,400	1.00	2.25	5.00	10.00	20.00	
1842	1,869,120	1.00	2.00	4.50	10.00	18.00	
1843 43 over 34	475,200	7.50	20.00	50.00	75.00	125.00	
1843		.80	1.75	4.00	8.00	15.00	
1860	160,000	1.50	5.00	10.00	20.00	37.50	
1862	256,000	1.50	5.00	10.00	19.00	35.00	
1870 Proof only		Very Rare					$450.00

SILVER TWOPENCES

Silver halfgroats or twopences dated 1838, 1843 and 1848 were struck for Colonial use. They cannot be distinguished from the regular Maundy coins. One or two other years may have been struck for use in the colonies. See listing under Maundy coins, page 103.

SILVER GROATS

The silver groat or fourpence was first coined at the suggestion of Joseph Hume to facilitate payment of the 4d. bus fare in London. The coin came to be known as the "Joey" because of its origin.

This denomination was used in British Guiana in large quantities to replace the old ¼ guilder that had been current there.

The reverse differs from that of the Maundy fourpence in that it shows Britannia seated, with the date in the exergue.

Diameter: 17.63mm; weight: 1.89 grams; composition: .925 silver, .075 copper; edge: reeded.

William IV 1830-1837

Date	Quantity Minted	Good	Fine	V. F.	Ex F.	Unc.	Proof
1836 4,253,040		$2.50	$5.00	$7.00	$12.00	$20.00	$70.00
1837 962,280		2.50	5.00	9.00	15.00	24.00	70.00

Victoria 1837-1901

Date	Quantity Minted	Good	Fine	V. F.	Ex F.	Unc.	Proof
1837 Proof or pattern only							200.00
1838		1.25	2.50	5.00	13.00	25.00	125.00
1838 8 over horz. 8 . . .	2,150,280	1.50	3.00	8.00	20.00	50.00	
1839 1,461,240		1.25	2.50	6.00	15.00	27.50	125.00
1840 1,496,880		1.25	2.50	5.00	14.00	26.00	
1841 344,520		1.50	3.00	8.00	20.00	35.00	
1842 2 over 1 . . .	724,680	1.50	3.00	8.00	20.00	40.00	
1842		1.25	2.50	6.00	15.00	27.50	125.00
1843 4 over 5 .	1,817,640	8.00	20.00	25.00	35.00	75.00	
1843		1.25	2.50	6.00	15.00	27.50	
1844 855,360		1.50	2.75	7.00	16.00	30.00	
1845 914,760		1.50	2.75	7.00	16.00	30.00	
1846 1,366,200		1.25	2.50	5.00	14.00	26.00	
1847 7 over 6 225,720		8.00	17.50	25.00	50.00	125.00	
1848 8 over 6 . . .	712,800	2.00	4.00	9.00	20.00	35.00	
1848 8 over 7 . . .		10.00	20.00	35.00	70.00	175.00	
1848		1.25	2.50	5.00	14.00	26.00	
1849 9 over 8 . . .	380,160	8.00	17.50	25.00	35.00	75.00	
1849		1.25	2.50	5.00	13.00	25.00	
1851 594,000		3.00	6.00	10.00	17.50	35.00	
1852 31,300		10.00	20.00	50.00	125.00	200.00	
1853 11,880		15.00	25.00	60.00	140.00	225.00	250.00
1854 1,096,613		1.25	2.50	5.00	14.00	26.00	
1855 741,081		1.25	2.50	5.00	14.00	26.00	
1857 Proof only							300.00
1862 Proof only							300.00

Jubilee Type

Issued solely for use in British Guiana and the West Indies.

Date	Quantity Minted	Good	Fine	V. F.	Ex F.	Unc.	Proof
1888 120,000		5.00	12.50	20.00	32.00	60.00	150.00

COINS OF GREAT BRITAIN
COPPER FARTHINGS

During the first ten years of the reign of George III no copper pieces were coined other than a small issue totaling £3,810, apparently all farthings, struck from dies of George II dated 1754.

In 1771, 1773, 1774 and 1775 copper farthings were struck for George III in the same style and weight as former years. Then followed a hiatus of twenty-two years during which time no regal copper coins were issued.

In 1797 a remarkable series of full intrinsic value copper penny and two-penny pieces was issued. Because of their size, they soon became known as "cartwheels." Proof farthings of this type were struck as pattern pieces, but this design was never adopted.

Matthew Boulton started making farthings of a slightly different design in 1799 at his Soho mint. The reverse of this coin has the inscription I.FARTH-ING around the lower edge. This was the first time that the name of a denomination is given on an English regal coin.

Perfect bright red uncirculated coins command higher prices.

George III 1760-1820

1799, diameter: 23.50mm; weight: 6.30 grams; composition: copper; edge: obliquely grained. *1806-7,* diameter: 21.50mm; weight: 6.02 grams.

Date	Good	Fine	V. F.	Ex. F.	Unc.
1799.........................	$ .85	$2.00	$4.00	$12.00	$20.00

1806.........................	.85	2.50	5.00	10.00	17.00
1807.........................	1.00	3.00	6.00	12.00	20.00

A total of £10,557 worth of farthings was coined by Boulton in the years 1799, 1806 and 1807. All dies were produced by Conrad Heinrich Küchler.

George IV 1820-1830

First Issue

The first issue of coins for George IV has a laureate bust of the king facing left. The obverse was designed by Benedetto Pistrucci and the reverse by William Wyon. The Roman numeral IIII was used on coins of the first issue from 1821 to 1826. This was replaced on the second issue by IV.

Diameter: 22mm; weight: 4.72 grams; composition: copper; edge: plain.

Date	Quantity Minted	Good	Fine	V. F.	Ex. F.	Unc.	Proof
1821 2,688,000		$ .75	$1.25	$3.00	$8.00	$20.00	$85.00
1822 5,924,352		.75	1.20	3.00	8.00	20.00	95.00
1823 . . . . }		.75	1.50	3.50	10.00	22.00	
1823 I for 1 . . . }2,365,440							
in date . . }		1.75	3.50	8.00	15.00	35.00	
1825 4,300,800		.75	1.25	3.00	8.00	20.00	
1826 6,666,240		1.50	3.00	7.00	12.00	25.00	

Perfect bright red uncirculated coins command higher prices.

Second Issue

In 1825 the king objected to the continuance of Pistrucci's portrait, which he found distasteful because of the puffed face, thick neck and wiry hair. William Wyon was commissioned to produce a new design, which was used on the farthings from 1826 to 1830.

1826 . . . . .inc. above		.60	1.00	3.00	10.00	20.00	85.00
1826 I for 1 in date		2.00	4.00	10.00	20.00	40.00	
1827 2,365,440		.80	1.50	5.00	20.00	35.00	
1828 2,365,440		.75	1.25	3.50	12.00	22.00	
1829 1,505,280		1.00	2.00	6.00	21.00	40.00	
1830 2,365,440		.75	1.25	3.50	12.00	25.00	

William IV 1830-1837

The portrait on the coins of William IV was engraved by William Wyon from a model by Sir Francis Chantrey.

1831 2,688,000		1.00	2.25	7.00	15.00	25.00	125.00
1834 1,935,360		.80	2.00	5.00	10.00	20.00	
1835 1,720,320		.80	2.00	5.00	10.00	20.00	
1836 1,290,240		1.00	2.25	7.00	15.00	27.50	
1837 3,010,560		.80	2.00	5.00	10.00	20.00	

Copper Farthings
Victoria 1837-1901

The heavyweight coins of Queen Victoria were designed by William Wyon, whose initials WW appear on the truncation of the neck. The reverse is his design of Britannia seated, first used during the reign of George IV, with REG substituted for REX.

The designer's initials WW are raised on coins issued from 1838 through 1852 and for some dated 1853 and 1855. The letters are incuse on all other farthings dated 1853-1860. Coins in this series are frequently found with letters and stops that are weak or missing due to the use of worn dies.

Copper farthings dated 1860 are not mentioned in the mint report and none was issued for circulation.

Diameter: 22mm; weight: 4.72 grams; composition: copper; edge: plain.

Young Head,
Copper Issue

Perfect bright red uncirculated coins command higher prices.

Date	Quantity Minted	Good	Fine	V. F.	Ex. F.	Unc.	Proof
1838	591,360	$1.00	$2.25	$4.00	$12.00	$25.00	
1839	4,300,800	.75	1.50	3.00	9.00	20.00	$90.00
1840	3,010,560	.75	1.50	3.00	9.00	20.00	
1841	1,720,320	.75	1.50	3.00	9.00	20.00	*125.00
1842	1,290,240	2.00	4.00	8.00	23.00	40.00	
1842 4 over ҍ		Rare					
1843	4,085,760	.50	1.25	2.75	8.00	18.00	
1843 I for 1 in date		2.00	3.50	7.00	15.00	27.50	
1844	430,080	8.00	15.00	25.00	60.00	175.00	
1845	3,225,600	1.00	2.25	4.00	10.00	23.00	
1846	2,580,480	2.00	4.00	7.50	22.00	37.50	
1847	3,879,720	1.00	1.75	3.00	9.00	22.00	
1848	1,290,240	1.00	1.75	3.00	9.00	22.00	
1849	645,120	5.00	10.00	20.00	50.00	80.00	
1850	430,080	2.00	3.50	7.00	15.00	27.50	
1851	1,935,360	3.00	7.00	14.00	35.00	60.00	
1851 DEI over ♉		6.00	12.00	22.00	50.00	100.00	
1852	822,528	4.00	8.00	18.00	40.00	75.00	
1853 3 over 2		20.00	50.00	80.00	125.00	300.00	
1853 w.w. raised	1,028,628	.50	1.00	2.00	7.00	17.00	125.00
1853 ww incuse		2.00	3.50	6.00	14.00	30.00	125.00
1854	6,504,960	.75	1.50	3.00	9.00	22.00	
1855 w.w. raised	3,440,640	1.00	2.50	5.00	18.00	30.00	
1855 ww incuse		1.00	2.50	5.00	20.00	35.00	
1856	1,771,392	2.00	4.00	10.00	30.00	50.00	
1856 E over R in VICTORIA		5.00	10.00	20.00	50.00	100.00	
1857	1,075,200	.75	1.50	3.00	9.00	22.00	
1858	1,720,320	.75	1.50	3.00	9.00	20.00	
1859	1,290,240	4.00	8.00	18.00	45.00	80.00	
1860			200.00	300.00	800.00	——	

*Proofs dated 1841 were probably restruck at the mint at a later date.

BRONZE FARTHINGS

In 1860 a new bronze coinage was adopted to replace the copper coins, which wore too rapidly for extensive circulation. The new, more durable, alloy was composed of 95 parts of copper, four of tin and one of zinc. The coins were also smaller and thinner, therefore more convenient to carry. The dies were engraved by Mr. Leonard Charles Wyon, then Engraver to the mint.

The earliest dies of 1860 have an outer circle of round beads. These apparently did not wear well and later in the year this border was replaced with a circle of elongated or toothed beads. Specimens dated 1860 with toothed obverse and beaded reverse exist.

Diameter: 20.16mm; weight: 2.83 grams; composition: .950 copper, .040 tin, .010 zinc; edge: plain.

Date	Quantity Minted	Good	Fine	V. F.	Ex. F.	Unc.	Proof
1860 beaded bdr..		$1.00	$3.00	$6.00	$15.00	$35.00	$125.00
1860 toothed bdr.	2,867,200	.25	.75	2.00	5.00	14.00	
1860 toothed obv., beaded rev..		20.00	50.00	80.00	125.00	300.00	
1861 8,601,600		.25	.75	2.50	6.00	15.00	125.00
1862 14,336,000		.25	.75	2.50	6.00	15.00	250.00
1863 1,433,600		15.00	30.00	60.00	90.00	250.00	*500.00
1864 2,508,800		.50	1.00	3.00	7.00	17.00	

1865 – 5 over 2   *1865 – Large 8*   *1865 – Small 8*

Date	Quantity Minted	Good	Fine	V. F.	Ex. F.	Unc.	Proof
1865 5 over 2		1.00	3.00	6.00	15.00	50.00	
1865 large 8	4,659,200	.25	.75	2.50	6.00	15.00	
1865 small 8		.25	.75	2.50	7.00	16.00	
1866 3,584,000		.20	.50	1.50	4.50	12.00	110.00
1867 5,017,600		.20	.50	1.75	5.00	14.00	110.00
1868 4,851,208		.20	.50	1.75	5.00	14.00	90.00
1869 3,225,600		1.00	2.00	4.00	10.00	30.00	
1872 2,150,400		.50	1.00	3.00	7.00	17.00	
1873 3,225,620		.20	.50	1.75	5.00	13.00	

*Proofs dated 1863 were probably struck at the mint at a later date.

During the 1870's and 1880's the mint was often working to full capacity. In some of these years much of the bronze coinage was manufactured, under government supervision, by Messrs. Ralph Heaton and Sons at Birmingham. These coins are distinguished by the presence of a small letter H below date.

There was a principal change in the portrait in 1874 when the nose was made more aquiline and the neck thicker. Further slight changes, such as a lower bridge to the nose and less wavy hair, were made in subsequent years up to 1883, after which the bust remained unaltered until the veiled head was substituted.

Bronze Farthings

The only major reverse changes were a reduction in the size of the date in 1875 and the addition of heraldic coloring lines to the shield of Britannia in 1881. On these coins the crosses on the shield are rendered in raised lines. The vertical hatchings (gules) signify red and the horizontal hatchings (azure) blue.

Perfect bright red uncirculated coins command higher prices.

Date	Quantity Minted	Good	Fine	V. F.	Ex. F.	Unc.	Proof
1874 H..........	} 3,584,000	$ .75	$1.50	$3.00	$6.00	$15.00	$175.00
1874 H Both G's over ᴐ ...		50.00	75.00	125.00	250.00	——	
1875 obv. of 1873 large date......712,760		6.00	15.00	23.00	37.50	125.00	
1875 obv. of 1873 small date...inc. above		10.00	25.00	35.00	50.00	175.00	
1875 obv. of 1874 small date...inc. above		8.00	20.00	30.00	45.00	150.00	
1875 H obv. of 1873.	} 6,092,800	Rare					
obv. of 1874.		.20	.50	1.50	4.50	12.00	150.00
1876 H..........1,175,200		4.00	10.00	18.00	35.00	100.00	
1877 Proofs were struck at a later date. None issued for circulation..							850.00
1878............4,008,540		.20	.50	1.50	4.00	10.00	175.00
1879 normal 9....	} 3,977,180	.20	.50	1.50	4.00	10.00	
1879 large 9.....		.50	1.00	2.25	6.00	15.00	
1880 four berries..	} 1,842,710	1.00	2.00	4.00	9.00	20.00	175.00
1880 three berries.		1.50	4.00	8.00	20.00	40.00	
1881............3,494,670		.20	.50	1.50	4.00	10.00	

Heaton mint mark below date.   *Heraldic color lines on shield.*

1881 shield heraldically colored. Proof only							500.00
1881 H..........1,792,000		1.00	2.00	4.00	8.00	18.00	
1882 H..........1,792,000		1.00	1.75	3.50	7.00	17.00	150.00
1883............1,128,680		1.50	3.00	6.00	15.00	30.00	175.00
1884............5,782,000		.20	.50	1.25	3.00	8.00	175.00
1885............5,442,308		.20	.50	1.25	3.00	8.00	175.00
1886............7,767,790		.20	.50	1.25	3.00	8.00	175.00
1887............1,340,800		1.00	1.75	3.50	7.00	16.00	
1888............1,887,250		.25	.50	1.50	4.00	10.00	
1889 A single specimen of this date has been reported.							
1890............2,133,070		.20	.50	1.50	4.00	10.00	175.00
1891............4,959,690		.20	.50	1.25	3.00	8.00	175.00
1892............887,240		2.00	5.00	9.00	25.00	75.00	200.00
1893............3,904,320		.20	.50	1.25	3.00	10.00	
1894............2,396,770		.20	.50	1.50	4.50	12.00	
1895...both types 2,852,852		5.00	12.00	20.00	35.00	125.00	

Note: HONI s(incuse), which appears on the edge of the mantle up to 1892 (often very indistinctly, owing to the worn state of many of the dies), disappears entirely from 1893 to 1895.

Veiled Head Issue

The dies for this issue were engraved by G. W. de Saulles. The obverse is from a model by Thomas Brock. The reverse is a modified copy of L. C. Wyon's design with the lighthouse and ship eliminated.

Most of the farthings dated 1897, and all those of subsequent dates up to and including 1917, were issued with a black finish so that they could be more readily distinguished from the half sovereign.

Diameter: 20.16mm; weight: 2.83 grams; composition: .950 copper, .040 tin, .010 zinc; edge: plain.

Date	Quantity Minted	Good	Fine	V. F.	Ex. F.	Unc.	Proof
1895	*2,852,852	$ .25	$ .50	$1.00	$3.00	$7.00	
1896	3,668,610	.25	.50	1.00	3.00	7.00	$100.00
1897 brilliant	} 4,579,800	.15	.25	.75	4.00	10.00	
1897 black		.15	.25	.75	2.00	5.00	
1898	4,010,080	.15	.25	.75	2.00	5.00	
1899	3,864,616	.15	.25	.75	2.25	6.00	
1900	5,969,317	.15	.25	.50	1.50	4.50	
1901	8,016,459	.15	.25	.50	1.50	3.50	

*A total of 2,852,852 farthings, both young head and veiled head, was minted in 1895.

Edward VII 1901-1910

No coins of King Edward were issued until 1902 when new dies were engraved by G. W. de Saulles, the Mint Engraver. The reverse of the farthings of 1903 was made from dies of the 1901 Victoria coins and shows the horizon in a slightly lower position than on all other varieties.

All of the regular issue farthings of Edward VII have the blackened finish that was first introduced in 1897 to distinguish them from the half sovereigns. The matte proof pieces of 1902 are not blackened.

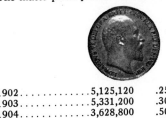

1902	5,125,120	.25	.50	1.25	2.50	6.50
1903	5,331,200	.30	.75	1.50	3.00	7.00
1904	3,628,800	.50	1.00	2.50	5.00	12.00
1905	4,076,800	.25	.50	1.50	3.00	7.00
1906	5,340,160	.20	.40	1.25	2.75	6.50
1907	4,399,360	.25	.50	1.50	3.00	7.00
1908	4,264,960	.25	.50	1.50	3.00	7.00
1909	8,852,480	.20	.40	1.25	2.50	6.00
1910	2,598,400	1.00	1.75	4.00	7.00	15.00

Bronze Farthings

George V 1910-1936

The portrait on the bronze farthings of George V was engraved by Sir Bertram Mackennal. The reverse was identical with that of the previous reign. With few alterations these dies were used until 1926 when a modified and very slightly smaller head is used. The designer's initials BM, on the truncation of the neck, were also made smaller and the periods eliminated. The reverse was also slightly altered.

The special blackened finish was discontinued and the bright finish was again used in 1918 and thereafter, when half sovereigns were no longer issued.

Diameter: 20.16mm; weight: 2.83 grams; composition: *1860-1922,* .950 copper, .040 tin, .010 zinc; *1923-1942,* .955 copper, .030 tin, .015 zinc; edge: plain.

1911-1925   1926-1936

Date	Quantity Minted	Good	Fine	V. F.	Ex. F.	Unc.	Proof
1911	5,196,800	$ .50	$ .75	$1.50	$2.50	$6.00	
1912	7,669,760	.25	.35	1.00	2.00	5.00	
1913	4,184,320	.35	.50	1.25	2.25	5.50	
1914	6,126,988	.35	.50	1.25	2.25	5.50	
1915	7,129,254	.75	1.00	2.25	4.00	12.00	
1916	10,993,325	.35	.50	1.25	2.00	5.00	
1917	21,434,844	.15	.30	.75	1.50	3.50	
1918	19,362,818	.15	.25	.50	1.00	2.50	
1919	15,089,425	.15	.25	.50	1.00	2.50	
1920	11,480,536	.15	.25	.50	1.00	3.00	
1921	9,469,097	.15	.25	.50	1.00	2.50	
1922	9,956,983	.15	.25	.50	1.00	2.50	
1923	8,034,457	.15	.25	.50	1.00	3.00	
1924	8,733,414	.15	.25	.50	1.00	2.75	
1925	12,634,697	.15	.25	.50	1.00	2.75	
1926	9,792,397	.15	.25	.50	1.00	3.00	$150.00
1927	7,868,355	.15	.25	.50	1.00	3.00	150.00
1928	11,625,600	.15	.25	.50	1.00	2.50	150.00
1929	8,419,200	.15	.25	.50	1.00	2.50	150.00
1930	4,195,200	.20	.30	1.00	1.50	3.50	150.00
1931	6,595,200	.15	.25	.50	1.00	2.50	150.00
1932	9,292,800	.15	.25	.50	1.00	2.00	150.00
1933	4,560,000	.20	.30	.80	1.25	3.00	150.00
1934	3,052,800	.25	.50	1.25	2.25	5.00	150.00
1935	2,227,200	.50	.75	1.50	3.00	7.00	200.00

Edward VIII 1936

Farthings dated 1936 were issued during the reign of King Edward VIII. All of these coins have the name and portrait of George V, because the mint did not have time to prepare coins with the portrait of King Edward before he abdicated the throne to marry an American, Mrs. Wallis Simpson.

1936	9,734,400	.15	.25	.60	1.20	3.00	200.00

George VI 1936-1952

A new reverse design was adopted for the farthing in 1937 mainly because of certain members of the Royal Mint Advisory Committee who favored a complete departure from the traditional design of former years. A number of artists were invited to submit designs and that of a wren, by H. Wilson Parker, was finally accepted.

In 1937, 1950 and 1951 proof strikings were issued in specimen sets. Proofs of other years are all extremely rare.

Diameter: 20.16mm; weight: 2.83 grams; composition: *1923-1942*, .955 copper, .030 tin, .015 zinc; *1942-1945*, .970 copper, .005 tin, .025 zinc; *1946-1956*, .955 copper, .030 tin, .015 zinc; edge: plain.

First Issue 1937-1948

Date	Quantity Minted Proof	Regular	V. Fine	Ex. F.	Unc.	Proof
1937	(26,402)	8,131,200	$ .25	$ .50	$1.75	$4.50
1938		7,449,600	.50	.80	3.00	
1939		31,440,000	.15	.25	1.00	
1940		18,360,000	.25	.50	1.50	
1941		27,312,000	.15	.25	1.25	
1942		28,857,600	.15	.25	1.25	
1943		33,345,600	.15	.25	1.00	
1944		25,137,600	.15	.25	1.00	
1945		23,736,000	.15	.25	1.00	
1946		24,364,800	.15	.25	1.00	
1947		14,745,600	.15	.25	1.00	
1948		16,622,400	.15	.25	1.00	

Second Issue 1949-1952

The words INDIAE IMPERATOR (Emperor of India) were omitted from the Royal Titles on all coinage after January 1, 1949. In the case of the farthings this necessitated the omission of IND:IMP. and the expansion of F:D: to FIDEI DEF.

1949		8,424,000	.15	.25	1.00	
1950	(17,513)	10,324,800	.15	.25	1.00	4.25
1951	(20,000)	14,016,000	.15	.25	1.00	4.25
1952		5,251,200	.20	.35	1.25	

Bronze Farthings

Elizabeth II 1952-

The Queen's portrait on these farthings was designed by Mrs. Mary Gillick. The original portrait was in very low relief and showed little detail in the hair and features. This defect was remedied by retouching the dies early in 1953. The reverse continues to use the wren designed by H. W. Parker for the farthings of George VI.

All of the farthings coined in 1952 have the name and portrait of George VI although they were issued during the reign of Elizabeth II.

Diameter: 20.16mm; weight: 2.83 grams; composition: .955 copper, .030 tin, .015 zinc; edge: plain.

First Issue 1953

Date	Quantity Minted Proof	Quantity Minted Regular	V. Fine	Ex. F.	Unc.	Proof
1953	(40,000)	6,109,200	$ .25	$ .50	$1.50	$4.00

Second Issue 1954-1956

In 1954 the dies were further retouched to sharpen the portrait and the legend was changed to eliminate BRITT: OMN: from the Queen's title.

Proof specimens struck during 1954-1956 are all extremely rare. The 1953 proofs were issued in specimen sets late in the year and all show the recut portrait.

1954	6,566,400	.10	.25	1.00
1955	5,779,200	.10	.20	1.00
1956	1,996,800	.75	1.25	3.00

No farthings were coined after 1956. The use of this denomination as a unit of currency was discontinued and all coins in circulation recalled effective January 1, 1961. Only a limited number, however, were immediately turned in at banks and returned to the mint for melting.

With the coinage of new pence and adoption of the decimal system commencing in 1971 all remaining farthings were removed from circulation.

COPPER HALFPENNIES

No copper coins bearing the portrait of George III were struck until 1770 although a small quantity of copper was coined in 1762 and 1763 from dies of George II dated 1754. The first official halfpennies for George III were dated 1770-1775. Most of these coins, however, were immediately melted and made into lightweight counterfeit halfpence.

In 1797 Matthew Boulton proposed to remedy this situation by coining copper pieces of nearly full intrinsic value. This resulted in the issuance of "cartwheel" penny and twopenny pieces coined by him at his Soho mint. These were the first English coins struck with steam power and a retaining collar to make them perfectly round and evenly struck.

Boulton prepared pattern "cartwheel" pieces in the denomination of one halfpenny but this design was never accepted. Later, in 1799, he began coinage of a halfpenny piece of slightly different design and weight. The faces of these coins are slightly concave to protect the design from wear and prevent counterfeiting.

George III 1760-1820

Diameter: 30.50mm; weight: 12.60 grams; composition: copper; edge: obliquely grained.

Perfect bright red uncirculated coins command higher prices.

Date	Good	Fine	V. F.	Ex. F.	Unc.
1799 ship has five guns..........	$ .75	$1.50	$3.50	$12.00	$30.00
1799 ship has six guns...........	.75	1.50	3.50	11.00	27.50
1799 ship has nine guns.........	.75	1.75	4.00	15.00	35.00

Diameter: 29mm; weight: 9.45 grams; composition: copper; edge: obliquely grained.

1806 no berries on olive branch...	.75	1.50	3.50	10.00	26.00
1806 three berries on olive branch.	.75	1.50	3.50	10.00	26.00
1807.............................	.75	1.50	4.00	12.00	30.00

A total of £357,869 worth of halfpennies was coined by Boulton at Soho in the years 1799, 1806 and 1807. The dies were produced by Conrad Heinrich Küchler, a talented Flemish die cutter.

Copper Halfpennies

George IV 1820-1830
Second Design

King George IV was never pleased with the portrait designed by Pistrucci for his coins. In 1824 William Wyon was commissioned to produce a new design which was used on most of the coins from 1825 to 1830. Halfpence of the Pistrucci design were never issued as only farthings were coined for the first five years of the reign.

Varieties of the reverse occur with either two incuse lines down the arms of the saltire, or one raised line.

Diameter: 28mm; weight: 9.45 grams; composition: copper; edge: plain.

Perfect bright red uncirculated coins command higher prices.

Date	Quantity Minted	Good	Fine	V. F.	Ex. F.	Unc.	Proof
1825 215,040		$4.00	$7.00	$15.00	$50.00	$100.00	$200.00
1826 9,031,630		1.00	2.00	6.00	15.00	30.00	150.00
1827 5,376,000		1.00	2.00	6.00	17.50	35.00	

William IV 1830-1837

The portrait on the coins of William IV was engraved by William Wyon from a model by Sir Francis Chantrey. The engraver's initials WW, incuse, are found on the truncation.

The mint report indicates that halfpennies were also coined in 1832, 1835 and 1836. These were undoubtedly struck from dies dated 1831 or 1834 and have been included in the following totals.

1831 806,400		1.00	2.00	6.00	17.50	35.00	90.00
1834 537,600		1.00	2.00	6.00	17.50	35.00	
1837 349,440		.75	1.50	5.00	15.00	30.00	

Victoria 1837-1901
Young Head, Copper Issue

The copper coins of Queen Victoria were designed by William Wyon, whose initials WW appear on the truncation of the neck. The reverse is his design of Britannia seated, first used during the reign of George IV, with REG substituted for REX.

This issue is notable for the number of pieces bearing altered dates struck from overcut dies of a previous year. This was done as a matter of economy to extend the life of lightly worn dies and involved only the last figure of the date.

Copper halfpennies dated 1860 are not mentioned in the mint report and none were issued for circulation. A few of the rare pieces are, however, known to exist. Some of them were restruck at the mint at a later date.

Diameter: 28mm; weight: 9.45 grams; composition: copper; edge: plain.

Perfect bright red uncirculated coins command higher prices.

Date	Quantity Minted	Good	Fine	V. F.	Ex. F.	Unc.	Proof
1838	456,960	$ .75	$1.50	$4.50	$8.50	$19.00	
1839	268,800						$175.00
1841	1,075,200	.50	1.00	3.25	6.00	16.00	100.00
1843	967,680	2.00	4.50	15.00	30.00	75.00	
1844	1,075,200	1.00	2.25	8.00	20.00	40.00	
1845	1,075,200	20.00	35.00	75.00	200.00	400.00	
1846	860,160	1.50	3.50	10.00	20.00	35.00	
1847	752,640	1.50	3.50	10.00	25.00	40.00	
1848 8 over 7	}322,560	1.50	3.50	11.00	25.00	40.00	
1848		1.50	3.50	12.00	27.50	45.00	
1851	}215,040	1.00	2.25	8.00	20.00	35.00	
1851 dots on shield		1.00	2.00	6.00	18.00	27.50	
1852	}637,056	1.50	3.50	11.00	22.00	37.50	
1852 dots on shield		1.50	3.50	12.00	25.00	40.00	
1853 3 over 2	}1,559,040	3.00	6.00	20.00	60.00	100.00	
1853		.50	1.00	3.25	6.00	16.00	125.00
1854	12,354,048	.50	1.00	3.25	6.00	16.00	
1855	1,455,837	.50	1.00	3.25	6.00	16.00	
1856	1,942,080	1.00	2.25	7.50	12.00	22.00	
1857	}1,182,720	.75	1.50	6.00	10.00	20.00	
1857 dots on shield		.50	1.00	4.50	8.00	16.00	
1858 8 over 6		1.00	2.00	8.00	15.00	35.00	
1858 8 over 7	}2,472,960	1.00	2.00	6.00	10.00	20.00	
1858 normal date		.50	1.00	4.00	7.00	17.00	
1858 small date		1.00	2.25	8.00	15.00	35.00	
1859 9 over 8	}1,290,240	1.50	3.50	12.00	27.50	50.00	
1859		1.00	2.50	8.00	15.00	40.00	
1860 Not issued for circulation							

Bronze Halfpennies

Young Head, Bronze Issue

In 1860 a new coinage of bronze was adopted to replace the copper coins, which wore too rapidly for extensive circulation. The new, more durable, alloy was composed of 95 parts of copper, four of tin and one of zinc. The coins were also smaller and thinner, therefore, more convenient to carry. The dies were engraved by Mr. Leonard Charles Wyon, then Engraver to the mint.

The earliest dies of 1860 have an outer circle of round beads. These apparently did not wear well and later in the year this border was replaced with a circle of elongated or toothed beads. All have toothed outer circles from 1861 onwards.

As the changeover from copper to bronze was to be made as quickly as possible, the demands on the mint were heavy and much of the new coinage was struck, under supervision, by Messrs. Boulton and Watt, and Messrs. Ralph Heaton and Sons, in Birmingham.

Rare varieties of the 1862 halfpenny are known with the letter A, B, or C between the base of the lighthouse and rim.

Diameter: 25.47mm; weight: 5.67 grams; composition: .950 copper, .040 tin, .010 zinc; edge: plain.

Beaded Border   Toothed Border   1861 HALF over HALP

Date	Quantity Minted	Good	Fine	V. F.	Ex. F.	Unc.	Proof
1860 beaded bdr..	}6,630,400	$ .50	$1.00	$3.00	$7.00	$16.00	
1860 toothed bdr..		.60	1.25	5.00	12.00	30.00	$175.00
1861 no signature		.50	1.00	3.00	7.00	15.00	100.00
1861 L.C.W. on rk.	}54,118,400	.50	1.00	3.00	7.00	17.00	
1861 same, wd/dt		.50	1.00	3.00	7.00	17.00	
1861 HALF over HALP.......		15.00	40.00	75.00	100.00	300.00	
1862...........61,107,200		.50	1.00	3.00	6.00	15.00	100.00
1863 normal 3...	}15,948,800	.75	2.00	6.00	15.00	35.00	
1863 large 3.....		.75	2.00	6.00	15.00	35.00	125.00
1864...............537,600		2.00	5.00	10.00	25.00	100.00	
1865 5 over 3.....	}8,064,000	20.00	50.00	100.00	125.00	350.00	
1865.............		2.50	6.00	12.00	30.00	60.00	
1866............2,508,800		2.00	5.00	10.00	25.00	50.00	150.00
1867............2,508,800		2.50	6.00	12.00	30.00	60.00	150.00
1868............3,046,400		2.25	5.50	11.00	27.50	55.00	100.00
1869............3,225,600		5.00	8.00	20.00	60.00	200.00	
1870............4,350,739		2.00	5.00	10.00	25.00	60.00	
1871............1,075,280		10.00	20.00	60.00	150.00	300.00	
1872............4,659,410		2.00	5.00	10.00	25.00	50.00	
1873............3,404,880		2.25	5.50	11.00	27.50	60.00	
1874....both var. 1,347,655		2.50	6.00	12.00	30.00	70.00	

Bronze Halfpennies

There was a principal change in the portrait in 1874 when the nose was made more aquiline and the neck thicker. Further slight changes were made in subsequent years up to 1883, after which the bust remained unaltered until the veiled head was substituted. The only major change in the reverse was the addition of heraldic coloring lines to the shield in 1881, where the crosses on the shield are rendered in raised lines. The vertical hatchings (gules) signify red and the horizontal hatchings (azure) blue.

During the 1870's and 1880's some of the bronze coinage was once again manufactured, under government supervision, by Messrs. Ralph Heaton and Sons at Birmingham. These coins bear a small letter H below the date.

Perfect bright red uncirculated coins command higher prices.

Date	Quantity Minted	Good	Fine	V. F.	Ex. F.	Unc.	Proof
1874..both var.	1,347,655	$2.00	$5.00	$10.00	$20.00	$45.00	
1874 H	5,017,600	1.00	2.00	5.00	12.00	30.00	$175.00
1875	5,430,815	1.00	2.00	5.00	12.00	30.00	
1875 H	1,254,400	2.00	5.00	10.00	20.00	45.00	
1876 H	5,809,600	1.00	2.00	4.00	10.00	25.00	
1877	5,209,505	1.00	2.00	4.00	10.00	25.00	150.00
1878	1,425,535	2.50	6.00	12.00	30.00	60.00	150.00
1879	3,582,545	.75	1.50	3.50	8.00	20.00	
1880	2,423,465	1.50	3.00	7.00	18.00	40.00	125.00
1881	2,007,515	1.00	2.00	6.00	15.00	35.00	

Heaton mint mark below date.   Heraldic color lines on shield.

Date	Quantity Minted	Good	Fine	V. F.	Ex. F.	Unc.	Proof
1881 shield heraldically colored. Proof only							800.00
1881 H	1,792,000	1.00	2.00	4.00	10.00	25.00	175.00
1882 H	4,480,000	.75	1.50	3.50	8.00	20.00	175.00
1883	3,000,725	1.00	2.00	4.00	10.00	25.00	100.00
1884	6,989,580	.50	1.00	3.00	7.00	16.00	100.00
1885	8,600,574	.50	1.00	3.00	7.00	15.00	100.00
1886	8,586,155	.50	1.00	3.00	7.00	15.00	100.00
1887	10,701,305	.35	.75	2.50	6.00	14.00	
1888	6,814,070	.50	1.00	3.00	7.00	16.00	
1889 9 over 8..	⎱7,748,234		50.00	100.00	200.00	——	
1889	⎰	.50	1.00	3.00	7.00	15.00	
1890	11,254,235	.35	.75	2.50	6.00	14.00	100.00
1891	13,192,260	.35	.75	2.50	6.00	14.00	100.00
1892	2,478,335	1.00	2.00	5.00	15.00	35.00	150.00
1893	7,229,344	.50	1.00	3.00	7.00	15.00	
1894	1,767,635	1.00	2.00	4.00	12.00	30.00	

Bronze Halfpennies

Veiled Head Issue

The dies for this issue were engraved by G. W. de Saulles. The obverse is from a model by Thomas Brock, whose initials TB appear below the shoulder. The reverse is a modified copy of L. C. Wyon's design, with the lighthouse and ship eliminated.

Date	Quantity Minted	Good	Fine	V. F.	Ex. F.	Unc.	Proof
1895	3,032,154	$ .35	$ .75	$1.25	$5.00	$10.00	
1896	9,142,500	.25	.50	1.00	4.00	8.00	
1897	8,690,315	.25	.50	1.00	4.00	8.00	
1898	8,595,180	.35	.75	1.25	5.00	9.00	
1899	12,108,001	.25	.40	.75	3.00	7.00	
1900	13,805,190	.25	.40	.75	3.00	7.00	
1901	11,127,360	.20	.30	.60	2.50	6.50	$125.00

Edward VII 1901-1910

The portrait for King Edward VII was the work of G. W. de Saulles, whose initials appear below the truncation of the neck. The reverse, showing a helmeted Britannia, is the same as was used on the last issue of halfpennies for Queen Victoria, except for slight modifications when the horizon was raised somewhat, late in 1902 and thereafter.

Date	Quantity Minted	Good	Fine	V. F.	Ex. F.	Unc.
1902 low horizon	13,672,960	2.00	10.00	15.00	40.00	75.00
high horizon		.20	.80	1.50	4.00	10.00
1903	11,450,880	.25	1.00	2.00	5.00	12.00
1904	8,131,200	.50	2.00	4.00	8.00	20.00
1905	10,124,800	.25	1.00	2.00	5.00	12.00
1906	11,101,440	.25	1.00	2.00	5.00	12.00
1907	16,849,280	.25	1.00	2.00	5.00	12.00
1908	16,620,800	.20	.80	1.50	5.00	12.00
1909	8,279,040	.35	1.50	3.00	7.00	17.50
1910	10,769,920	.25	1.00	2.00	5.00	12.00

George V 1910-1936

The dies for the halfpennies of this reign were engraved by Sir Bertram Mackennal. His initials B.M. are on the truncation of the bust. The first reverse is identical with that used in previous years. Many of the bronze blanks used for these coins were produced by private firms in Birmingham.

A great deal of difficulty was encountered in striking coins of this design. The high relief portrait caused a displacement of metal, called "ghosting," that showed through on the reverse side as an incuse outline of the head.

A new bronze alloy was adopted in 1923 in an effort to remedy the situation. It consisted of 95.5 per cent copper, 3 per cent tin and 1.5 per cent zinc. This alloy has a more golden tint than the former one. It lessened the hardness, enabled the coins to be more easily struck and lengthened the life of the dies.

Diameter: 25.47mm; weight: 5.67 grams; composition: *1860-1922*, .950 copper, .040 tin, .010 zinc; *1923-1942*, .955 copper, .030 tin, .015 zinc; edge: plain.

First Head 1911-early 1925

Date	Quantity Minted	Fine	V. Fine	Ex. Fine	Unc.	Proof
1911................12,570,880		$ .75	$1.75	$4.00	$8.50	
1912................21,185,920		.50	1.25	3.50	7.50	
1913................17,476,480		.75	2.00	5.00	10.00	
1914................20,289,111		.50	1.25	3.50	7.50	
1915................21,563,040		.75	1.75	4.50	9.00	
1916................39,386,143		.25	.75	3.00	7.00	
1917................38,245,436		.25	.75	3.00	7.00	
1918................22,321,072		.25	.75	3.00	7.00	
1919................28,104,001		.25	.75	3.00	7.00	
1920................35,146,793		.25	.75	3.00	7.00	
1921................28,027,293		.75	1.75	4.00	8.00	
1922................10,734,964		.75	2.00	5.00	10.00	
1923................12,266,282		.75	1.75	4.00	8.00	
1924................13,971,038		.50	1.25	3.50	7.50	
1925........both var. 12,216,123		.75	2.00	5.00	10.00	

During 1925 the features of the design were slightly modified to further help eliminate the "ghosting," but this fault was not fully corrected until 1928 when a new design, with a smaller head, was introduced.

The coins with the modified effigy from late 1925 and thereafter all have the designer's initials in small letters without periods.

Bronze Halfpennies

Halfpennies with the modified effigy can be distinguished by the hair which is depicted by faintly incuse lines, and the eyelid which curves downward to the right where previously it was straight. There is a pupil in the eye, and the underside of the nose has a more upward curve. On the reverse the exergual line has been raised slightly, the size of the border denticals increased, and the rim is thicker.

Modified Effigy 1925-1927

Date	Quantity Minted	Fine	V. F.	Ex. F.	Unc.	Proof
1925 modified effigy.............		$ .85	$2.25	$6.00	$12.00	
1926.................6,712,306		.75	2.00	5.00	10.00	$100.00
1927.................15,589,622		.25	.75	3.00	7.00	80.00

Small Head 1928-1936

1928.................20,935,200		.25	.75	3.00	6.00	100.00
1929.................25,680,000		.25	.75	3.00	6.00	100.00
1930.................12,532,800		.25	.75	3.00	6.00	100.00
1931.................16,137,600		.25	.75	3.00	6.00	100.00
1932.................14,448,000		.30	1.00	4.00	8.00	100.00
1933.................10,560,000		.25	.75	3.00	6.00	100.00
1934.................7,704,000		.50	1.50	6.00	10.00	100.00
1935.................12,180,000		.30	1.00	4.00	8.00	100.00

Edward VIII 1936

Halfpennies dated 1936 were issued during the reign of King Edward VIII. All of these coins have the name and portrait of George V due to the fact that the mint did not have time to begin coinage before he abdicated the throne in December of 1936.

1936.................23,008,800		.20	.50	2.50	5.00	120.00

George VI 1936-1952

The traditional Britannia reverse was not used on the bronze coinage of King George VI. Both the obverse and reverse of the halfpenny were designed by T. Humphrey Paget. The striking reverse design shows Sir Francis Drake's ship, the Golden Hind. Paget's initials HP are in the field below the stern. In 1937, 1950 and 1951 proof strikings were issued in specimen sets. Proofs of other years are all very rare.

Diameter: 25.47mm; weight: 5.67 grams; composition: *1923-1942*, .955 copper, .030 tin, .015 zinc; *1942-1945*, .970 copper, .005 tin, .025 zinc; *1946-1952*, .955 copper, .030 tin, .015 zinc; edge: plain.

First Issue 1937-1948

Date	Quantity Minted Proof	Quantity Minted Regular	V. Fine	Ex. F.	Unc.	Proof
1937	(26,402)	24,504,000	$ .25	$ .75	$2.50	$8.00
1938		40,320,000	.25	1.00	3.00	
1939		28,924,800	.50	1.50	5.00	
1940		32,162,400	.50	2.00	6.00	
1941		45,120,000	.25	.75	2.50	
1942		71,908,000	.20	.50	2.00	
1943		76,200,000	.20	.50	2.00	
1944		81,840,000	.20	.50	2.00	
1945		57,000,000	.25	.75	2.50	
1946		22,725,600	.75	3.50	8.00	
1947		21,266,400	.25	1.25	4.00	
1948		26,947,200	.25	.75	2.50	

Second Issue 1949-1952

Halfpennies of the second issue, 1949-1952, have obverse legend in slightly thicker letters, and terminating REX FIDEI DEF., the words IND: IMP. being omitted.

1949		24,744,000	.30	1.00	3.00	
1950	(17,513)	24,153,600	.30	1.00	3.50	6.50
1951	(20,000)	14,868,000	.50	1.50	4.50	6.50
1952		33,278,400	.30	1.00	3.00	

[33]

Bronze Halfpennies

Elizabeth II 1952-

The portrait for the coinage of Queen Elizabeth was designed by Mrs. Mary Gillick. Her initials MG appear on the center of the truncation of the shoulder. The ship design first used on the George VI halfpennies continued in use on these coins.

Diameter: 25.47mm; weight: 5.67 grams; composition: *1953-1959,* .955 copper, .030 tin, .015 zinc; *1959-1967,* .970 copper, .005 tin, .025 zinc; edge: plain.

First Issue 1953

Date	Quantity Minted Proof	Regular	Ex. F.	Unc.	Proof
1953	(40,000)	8,910,000	$1.25	$3.50	$6.50

The original portrait was in very low relief and showed little detail in the hair. This defect was remedied by retouching the dies during 1953. In 1954 the dies were further retouched to sharpen the portrait and the legend was changed to eliminate BRITT:OMN: from the Queen's title.

Proof specimens struck from 1954 to 1967 are all extremely rare. The 1953 proofs were issued in specimen sets late in the year; all show the recut portrait.

Second Issue 1954-1970

Date	Regular	Ex. F.	Unc.	Proof
1954	19,375,200	1.50	5.00	
1955	18,465,600	1.25	4.00	
1956	21,799,200	1.50	6.00	
1957	39,672,000	.50	1.50	
1958	66,331,200	.25	.90	
1959	79,176,000	.20	.75	
1960	41,340,000	.20	.75	
1962	41,779,200	.15	.50	
1963	42,720,000	.15	.50	
1964	78,583,200	.15	.40	
1965	98,083,200	.15	.40	
1966	95,289,600	.15	.40	
1967	146,491,400	.10	.35	
1970 issued only in sets				1.50

COPPER PENNIES

In 1797 a remarkable series of full intrinsic value copper penny and two-penny pieces was issued. Because of their size, they soon became known as "cartwheels."

On June 9, 1797, the Government signed a contract with Matthew Boulton providing for the coinage of 20 tons of twopences and 480 tons of pennies. The coins were made current July 26, 1797, and the one penny piece was to weigh one ounce avoirdupois and correspond as nearly as possible to its nominal value. They were to be legal tender up to one shilling. A total of £310,885 worth of pennies was coined between 1797 and 1807 by Boulton at the Soho mint. Conrad H. Küchler was the designer. The unique piece dated 1808 was formerly in the Boulton estate.

George III 1760-1820

Diameter: 35.80mm; weight: 28.35 grams; composition: copper; edge: plain.

The "Cartwheel" Penny of 1797

Date	Quantity Minted	Good	Fine	V. F.	Ex. F.	Unc.	Proof
1797	8,601,600	$3.00	$6.00	$17.00	$50.00	$100.00	——

Diameter: 34mm; weight: 18.90 grams; composition: copper; edge: obliquely grained.

Perfect bright red uncirculated coins command higher prices.

Date		Good	Fine	V. F.	Ex. F.	Unc.	Proof
1806		1.50	2.50	5.00	15.00	30.00	$100.00
1807		1.50	2.50	7.00	17.50	35.00	110.00
1808 (Unique)						——	

Copper Pennies

George IV 1820-1830
Second Design

Only copper farthings were coined during the first five years of the reign of King George IV. These coins were designed by Pistrucci and as the portrait was not pleasing to the King, William Wyon was commissioned to produce a new design which was used on most of the coins from 1825 to 1830. Coins of the second issue, by Wyon, show a much more pleasing portrait.

Diameter: 30.81mm; weight: 18.90 grams; composition: copper; edge: plain.

Date	Quantity Minted	Good	Fine	V. Fine	Ex. Fine	Unc.	Proof
1825	1,075,200	$2.25	$6.00	$15.00	$50.00	$100.00	$250.00
1826	5,913,600	2.00	5.00	10.00	35.00	70.00	200.00
1827	1,451,520	15.00	50.00	125.00	250.00	500.00	

Perfect bright red uncirculated coins command higher prices.

William IV 1830-1837

The portrait on the coins of William IV was engraved by William Wyon from a model by Sir Francis Chantrey. Mint reports indicate that pennies were also coined in 1832, 1835 and 1836. No coins with these dates are known to exist and undoubtedly dies dated 1831 or 1834 were used. These coinage figures have been included in the following totals.

A variety of 1831 has the engraver's initials WW on the truncation.

Date	Quantity Minted	Good	Fine	V. Fine	Ex. Fine	Unc.	Proof
1831 with ww	806,400	2.25	6.00	25.00	70.00	125.00	
1831		2.25	6.00	15.00	40.00	80.00	200.00
1834	322,560	2.25	7.00	20.00	50.00	100.00	
1837	174,720	5.00	10.00	35.00	100.00	200.00	

Victoria 1837-1901
Young Head, Copper Issue

This coin was designed by William Wyon, whose initials W. W., incuse, appear on the truncation from 1839 to 1858. Some pennies dated 1858 and those of 1859-1860 do not have these initials.

The reverse is his design of Britannia seated, first used during the reign of George IV, with REG substituted for REX.

This issue is notable for the number of pieces bearing altered dates struck from overcut dies of a previous year. This was done as a matter of economy to extend the life of lightly worn dies. The alteration on the die usually involved only the last figure of the date.

The normal position of the last colon is midway between F and Britannia's foot (DEF :) and this occurs for every date. For the years 1846, 1847, 1851 and 1853 to 1857, specimens also occur with the colon close to F (DEF:). In 1841 and 1843 specimens occur both with and without the colon after REG.

Mint records list 263,424 pence struck in 1852. These were undoubtedly all coins dated 1851 and have been included in the 1851 listing.

Diameter: 34mm; weight: 18.90 grams; composition: copper; edge: plain.

Perfect bright red uncirculated coins command higher prices.

Date	Quantity Minted	Good	Fine	V. F.	Ex. F.	Unc.	Proof
1839 bronzed proofs only							$175.00
1841 REG:	913,920	$3.00	$7.00	$15.00	$35.00	$60.00	175.00
1841 REG		1.00	2.00	7.00	18.00	30.00	
1843 REG:	483,840	10.00	20.00	50.00	125.00	200.00	
1843 REG		10.00	20.00	60.00	150.00	250.00	
1844...........215,040		2.00	5.00	10.00	20.00	40.00	
1845...........322,560		3.50	9.00	20.00	50.00	80.00	
1846 DEF : ...	483,840	2.00	6.00	12.00	25.00	50.00	
1846 DEF:		2.00	6.00	14.00	30.00	60.00	
1847 DEF : ...	430,080	2.00	5.00	10.00	20.00	40.00	
1847 DEF:		2.00	5.00	10.00	20.00	40.00	
1848 8 over 6...	161,280	3.00	8.00	20.00	60.00	90.00	
1848 8 over 7...		2.00	7.00	15.00	32.00	60.00	
1848..........		2.00	6.00	12.00	25.00	50.00	
1849...........268,800		17.50	35.00	100.00	200.00	300.00	

Copper Pennies

Date	Quantity Minted	Good	Fine	V. F.	Ex. F.	Unc.	Proof
1851 DEF : ...	} 532,224	$2.00	$6.00	$12.00	$25.00	$50.00	
1851 DEF: ...		2.00	6.00	14.00	30.00	65.00	
1853 DEF : ...	} 1,021,440	.75	1.50	4.00	14.00	24.00	$175.00
1853 DEF: ...		.75	1.50	6.00	18.00	30.00	
1854 4 over 3..		5.00	10.00	20.00	80.00	175.00	
1854 DEF : ...	} 6,720,000	.75	1.50	6.00	18.00	30.00	
1854 DEF: ...		.75	1.50	5.00	14.00	25.00	
1855 DEF : ...	} 5,273,856	.75	1.50	6.00	18.00	30.00	
1855 DEF: ...		.75	1.50	5.00	14.00	25.00	
1856 DEF : ...	} 1,212,288	5.00	12.00	25.00	80.00	170.00	
1856 DEF: ...		5.00	10.00	20.00	70.00	150.00	200.00
1857 DEF : ...	} 752,640	.75	1.50	6.00	20.00	40.00	
1857 DEF:		.75	1.50	6.00	18.00	30.00	
1857 sm. date...		1.50	4.00	10.00	25.00	50.00	
(1858 All kinds 1,559,040)							
1858 8 over 3..........		Rare					
1858 8 over 6..........		Rare					
1858 8 over 7..........		.75	1.50	5.00	15.00	27.50	
1858 small date........		2.00	6.00	12.00	25.00	50.00	
1858 without w.w.		.75	1.50	5.00	14.00	25.00	
1858.................		.75	1.50	5.00	14.00	24.00	
1859.........	} 1,075,200	1.00	2.00	7.00	18.00	30.00	
1859 sm. date.		1.50	4.00	10.00	22.00	42.00	
1860 60 over 59...32,256		75.00	100.00	200.00	350.00	600.00	

Victoria Pennies — Second Issue
Bronze, Young Head, 1860-1894

In 1860 a new coinage of bronze was adopted to replace the copper coins, which wore too rapidly for extensive circulation. The new, more durable, alloy was composed of 95 parts of copper, four of tin and one of zinc. The coins were also smaller and thinner, therefore, more convenient to carry. The dies were engraved by Leonard Charles Wyon, then Engraver to the mint.

The earliest dies of 1860 have an outer circle of round beads. These apparently did not wear well and later in the year this border was replaced with a circle of elongated or toothed beads. A few specimens dated 1860 with toothed obverse and beaded reverse are reported to exist. All have toothed outer circles from 1861 onwards.

Beaded Borders

Toothed Borders

As the changeover from copper to bronze was to be made as quickly as possible, the demands on the mint were heavy and much of the new coinage was struck, under supervision, by Messrs. Boulton and Watt, and Messrs. Ralph Heaton and Sons, in Birmingham. In 1874 and thereafter the Heaton coinage has a small H beneath the date.

Several varieties occur in the placement of the engraver's signature on the pennies of 1860 and 1861. The Queen's portrait was changed slightly in 1874 and again in 1881 to show a gradual aging of the features. Heraldic coloring lines were added to the shield of Britannia in 1881. On these coins the crosses on the shield are rendered in raised lines. The vertical hatchings (gules) signify red and the horizontal hatchings (azure) blue.

Rare varieties of the 1863 penny are known with the number 2, 3, or 4 below the date.

Diameter: 30.81mm; weight: 9.45 grams; composition: .950 copper, .040 tin, .010 zinc; edge: plain.

Date	Quantity Minted	Good	Fine	V. F.	Ex. F.	Unc.	Proof
(1860 All kinds.....5,053,440)							
1860 beaded borders..........		$ .75	$1.50	$6.00	$15.00	$40.00	$175.00
1860 toothed borders, L.C.W. below foot........		1.00	2.00	10.00	20.00	60.00	
1860 similar, L.C.W. below shield...........		.50	1.00	5.00	12.00	25.00	175.00
1860 similar, no L.C. Wyon on obverse............		.50	1.00	5.00	14.00	30.00	
(1861 All kinds....36,449,280)							
1861 signature on obv. and rev.		.75	1.50	6.00	15.00	32.50	
1861 no sig. on obv. or rev....		.50	1.00	5.00	12.00	25.00	175.00
1861 signature on obv. only...		.75	1.50	6.00	15.00	35.00	
1861 signature on rev. only....		.50	1.00	5.00	12.00	25.00	
1861 6 of date over 8.........							
1862 normal date.. } 50,534,400		.50	1.00	4.00	10.00	21.00	225.00
1862 small date.... }							
1863.............28,062,720		.50	1.00	4.00	10.00	22.50	225.00
1864 plain 4........ } 3,440,640		8.00	12.00	30.00	120.00	225.00	
1864 crosslet 4...... }		10.00	15.00	40.00	175.00	300.00	
1865 5 over 3....... } 8,601,600		10.00	15.00	40.00	175.00	400.00	
1865.............. }		3.00	8.00	20.00	35.00	100.00	
1866.............9,999,360		1.50	3.00	8.00	16.00	40.00	
1867.............5,483,520		3.00	8.00	20.00	35.00	100.00	350.00
1868.............1,182,720		4.00	10.00	25.00	75.00	150.00	225.00
1869.............2,580,480		20.00	50.00	125.00	350.00	700.00	
1870.............5,695,022		3.00	8.00	20.00	35.00	100.00	

Bronze Pennies

Date	Quantity Minted	Good	Fine	V. F.	Ex. F.	Unc.	Proof
1871	1,290,318	$5.00	$12.00	$32.50	$150.00	$250.00	
1872	8,494,572	1.00	2.75	7.00	15.00	40.00	
1873	8,494,200	1.00	2.50	6.00	14.00	30.00	
1874 style of 1873	5,621,865	2.00	5.00	10.00	20.00	60.00	
1874 new portrait		2.00	5.00	10.00	20.00	60.00	
1874 H style 1873	6,666,240	1.75	4.50	9.00	18.00	50.00	
1874 H new port		1.75	4.50	9.00	18.00	50.00	$175.00
1875	10,691,040	1.00	2.50	6.00	14.00	35.00	175.00
1875 H	752,640	12.00	25.00	70.00	200.00	500.00	——
1876 H	11,074,560	1.50	3.00	8.00	15.00	40.00	
1876 Two specimens without H have been reported.							
1877	9,624,747	1.00	2.50	6.00	14.00	30.00	350.00
1878	2,764,470	3.00	8.00	20.00	35.00	100.00	300.00
1879	7,666,476	1.00	2.50	6.00	14.00	30.00	
1880	3,000,831	3.00	8.00	20.00	35.00	90.00	200.00
1881 style of 1880	2,302,362	4.00	10.00	22.00	40.00	100.00	225.00
1881 new portrait		4.00	10.00	22.00	50.00	120.00	225.00

Date	Quantity Minted	Good	Fine	V. F.	Ex. F.	Unc.	Proof
1881 shield heraldically colored. Proof only							——
1881 H	3,763,200	2.00	5.00	10.00	20.00	50.00	175.00
1882	V. Rare		——	——	——		
1882 H	7,526,400	1.50	3.00	8.00	15.00	40.00	200.00
1883	6,237,438	1.50	3.00	8.00	15.00	40.00	175.00
1884	11,702,802	1.00	2.50	6.00	14.00	30.00	150.00
1885	7,145,862	1.00	2.50	6.00	14.00	30.00	150.00
1886	6,087,759	1.50	3.00	8.00	15.00	40.00	150.00
1887	5,315,085	.50	1.00	5.00	12.00	25.00	
1888	5,125,020	1.50	3.00	8.00	15.00	40.00	
1889	12,559,737	.50	1.00	4.00	10.00	20.00	
1890	15,330,840	.50	1.00	4.00	10.00	20.00	175.00
1891	17,885,961	.50	1.00	4.00	10.00	20.00	175.00
1892	10,501,671	.50	1.00	4.00	10.00	20.00	175.00
1893	8,161,737	.50	1.00	4.00	10.00	20.00	
1894	3,883,452	2.00	5.00	10.00	20.00	45.00	

Perfect bright red uncirculated coins command higher prices.

Victoria Pennies — Third Issue
Bronze, Veiled Head, 1895-1901

These dies were engraved by G. W. de Saulles; the obverse from a model by Thomas Brock, whose initials appear below the bust; the reverse copied, with minor modifications, from that of L. C. Wyon.

Date	Quantity Minted	Good	Fine	V. F.	Ex. F.	Unc.	Proof
1895 missing sea..	⎫ 5,395,830	$4.00	$10.00	$25.00	$125.00	$225.00	$300.00
1895 with sea....	⎭	1.00	2.00	4.00	10.00	18.00	150.00
1896 24,147,156		.50	1.00	3.00	6.00	12.00	
1897 20,756,620		.50	1.00	3.00	6.00	12.00	
1898 14,296,836		1.00	2.00	4.50	12.00	20.00	
1899 26,441,069		.50	1.00	3.00	6.00	12.00	
1900 31,778,109		.30	.75	2.50	5.00	10.00	
1901 22,205,568		.25	.50	1.50	4.00	8.00	200.00

Perfect bright red uncirculated coins command higher prices.

Edward VII 1901-1910

Coins of Edward VII were first issued in 1902. Mint Engraver G. W. de Saulles produced these dies. His initials De S. are beneath the bust. The reverse die used on some of the 1902 pennies is the type of the 1901 penny of Victoria. It shows the horizon in a slightly lower position than on the other coins in this series.

Diameter: 30.81mm; weight: 9.45 grams; composition: .950 copper, .040 tin, .010 zinc; edge: plain.

		Good	Fine	V.F.	Ex.F.	Unc.
1902 low horizon	⎫	1.75	2.50	6.00	20.00	60.00
1902 normal horizon	⎬ 26,976,768	.30	.75	2.50	5.00	12.00
1903 21,415,296		.75	1.50	4.00	8.00	17.00
1904 12,913,152		1.00	2.00	5.00	10.00	20.00
1905 17,783,808		.75	1.50	4.00	8.00	17.00
1906 37,989,504		.50	1.00	3.00	6.00	12.00
1907 47,322,240		.25	.50	2.00	4.00	10.00
1908 31,506,048		.50	1.00	3.00	6.00	12.00
1909 19,617,024		.70	1.25	3.50	7.00	15.00
1910 29,549,184		.50	1.00	3.00	6.00	12.00

Bronze Pennies

George V 1910-1936

The bronze coinage of George V began in 1911. Sir Bertram Mackennal designed the obverse. The reverse is the same as that of the previous reign. The design was slightly modified during the period 1925-1928. A new, smaller head was adopted in 1928.

During 1912, 1918 and 1919 some of the pennies were struck by the Mint, Birmingham, Ltd., (marked H) and during 1918 and 1919 by the Kings Norton Metal Co., Ltd., (marked KN). Pennies dated 1933 were not issued for circulation. A few special strikings were made and these coins were placed in cornerstones and museum collections.

Diameter: 30.81mm; weight: 9.45 grams; composition: *1860-1922*, .950 copper, .040 tin, .010 zinc; *1923-1940*, .955 copper, .030 tin, .015 zinc; edge: plain.

Date	Quantity Minted	Good	Fine	V. F.	Ex. F.	Unc.	Proof
1911	23,079,168	$ .30	$ .75	$1.50	$7.00	$15.00	
1912	48,306,048	.30	.75	1.50	7.50	16.00	
1912 H	16,800,000	1.00	2.00	5.00	20.00	40.00	
1913	65,497,872	.30	.75	1.50	7.50	16.50	
1914	50,820,997	.30	.75	1.50	7.50	16.00	
1915	47,310,807	.30	.75	1.75	8.00	17.50	
1916	86,411,165	.25	.70	1.25	6.00	14.00	
1917	107,905,436	.25	.70	1.00	5.00	12.00	

Heaton Mint

Kings Norton Mint

Date	Quantity Minted	Good	Fine	V. F.	Ex. F.	Unc.	Proof
1918	84,227,372	.30	.75	1.50	7.00	15.00	
1918 H	3,660,800	1.50	4.00	10.00	50.00	100.00	
1918 KN		3.00	6.00	15.00	80.00	200.00	
1919	113,761,090	.25	.70	1.00	5.00	12.00	
1919 H	5,209,600	1.25	3.50	9.00	40.00	120.00	
1919 KN		4.00	8.00	16.00	100.00	350.00	
1920	124,693,485	.20	.50	.75	4.00	10.00	

Diameter: 30.81mm; weight: 9.45 grams; composition: *1923-1940*, .955 copper, .030 tin, .015 zinc; *1944-1945*, .970 copper, .005 tin, .025 zinc; *1946-1951*, .955 copper, .030 tin, .015 zinc; edge: plain.

Modified Head 1926-1927

Date	Quantity Minted	Fine	V. Fine	Ex. Fine	Unc.	Proof
1921	129,717,693	$ .50	$ .75	$4.00	$10.00	
1922	16,346,711	.75	2.00	10.00	25.00	
1926	} 4,498,519	1.00	3.00	15.00	32.00	$200.00
1926 modified head		10.00	50.00	100.00	200.00	———
1927	60,989,561	.50	.75	4.00	10.00	200.00

Small Head 1928-1936

1928	50,178,000	.25	.50	3.00	8.00	200.00
1929	49,132,800	.25	.50	3.00	8.00	200.00
1930	29,097,600	.50	.80	5.00	12.00	200.00
1931	19,843,200	.70	1.25	7.00	15.00	200.00
1932	8,277,600	1.00	3.00	15.00	30.00	200.00
1933	8	Not issued for circulation.				
1934	13,965,600	.75	1.75	8.00	17.50	200.00
1935	56,070,000	.25	.50	2.50	6.50	200.00

Most of the pennies of 1934 and 1935 were issued artificially toned at the mint to discourage use as gifts. Brilliant red uncirculated specimens are more valuable than the toned.

Edward VIII 1936

Pennies dated 1936 were issued during this short reign; however, they all have the name and portrait of George V due to the fact that the mint did not start production of Edward VIII type coins before his abdication.

1936	154,296,000	.25	.50	2.50	6.50	150.00

Bronze Pennies

George VI 1936-1952

Coinage of pennies for domestic use was unnecessary during 1941-1943. Pennies issued during this period for Gibraltar and the West Indies were all dated 1940. The demand for pennies increased between 1944 and 1948, but in 1949 coinage was once again stopped and only small quantities were struck, using the 1949 dies, for the next seven years. A few pennies dated 1950 and 1951 were struck, mostly for inclusion in specimen sets. Proof specimens dated 1938 through 1949 are all extremely rare. In 1948 the words INDIAE IMPERATOR were dropped from the Royal Titles. The pennies of 1949 and thereafter show this change. The issues of 1944, 1945 and 1946 were chemically darkened at the mint with hyposulphite to prevent hoarding of bright new pennies.

The reverse design of 1937-1940 has a single exergual line. Sometime during coinage of the 1940 pennies, and continuing thereafter, this was changed to a double line.

1937-1948

Date	Quantity Minted Proof	Quantity Minted Regular	V. F.	Ex. F.	Unc.	Proof
1937	(26,402)	88,896,000	$ .50	$1.25	$3.50	$12.00
1938		121,560,000	.50	1.50	5.00	
1939		55,560,000	.75	2.25	7.00	
1940		42,284,400	1.25	3.50	10.00	
1944		42,600,000	.75	2.25	7.50	
1945		79,531,200	.75	2.25	7.00	
1946		66,855,600	.50	1.50	6.00	
1947		52,220,400	.30	.90	3.00	
1948		63,961,200	.30	.90	3.00	

1949-1951

Date	Proof	Regular	V. F.	Ex. F.	Unc.	Proof
1949		14,324,400	.50	1.25	3.25	
1950	(17,513)	240,000	7.00	15.00	35.00	35.00
1951	(20,000)	120,000	15.00	20.00	35.00	35.00

Elizabeth II 1952-

These coins were designed by Mrs. Mary Gillick. Her initials MG appear on the raised edge of the shoulder. Pennies were struck during 1952 but were all dated 1953. No pennies were struck for circulation dated 1954, although a few trial pieces were made. Coinage of this denomination was suspended until 1961 because of a surplus of these coins held in reserve. Those dated 1970 were issued only in sets.

After decimalization nearly half of the pennies thought to be in circulation were withdrawn. Many were disposed of to refiners, and those containing $\frac{1}{2}\%$ tin were used to produce new bronze coins.

Diameter: 30.81mm; weight: 9.45 grams; composition: *1953*, .955 copper, .030 tin, .015 zinc; *1961-1967*, .970 copper, .005 tin, .025 zinc; edge: plain.

Date	Quantity Minted Proof	Regular	V. F.	Ex. F.	Unc.	Proof
1953	(40,000)	1,308,400	$1.75	$3.00	$7.50	$12.00

The obverse legend on all British coins was changed in 1954 to eliminate BRITT:OMN: from the Queen's title.

BRITT:OMN: *Omitted*

Date	Quantity	V.F.	Unc.	Proof
1954..........................	(Unique)	Not issued for circulation.		
1961........................	48,313,400	.50	1.25	
1962........................	157,588,600	.20	.75	
1963........................	119,733,600	.15	.50	
1964........................	153,294,000	.15	.50	
1965........................	121,310,400	.15	.50	
1966........................	165,739,200	.15	.35	
1967........................	325,670,807	.15	.35	
1970 issued only in sets.................				2.00

[45]

COPPER TWOPENCE
George III 1760-1820

Between 1770 and the end of the century the practice of counterfeiting became so prevalent in England that scarcely any genuine British copper coins remained in circulation. The 1770-1775 issue was melted in huge quantities and made into lightweight counterfeit coins; the only other pieces in circulation were the merchants' tokens issued by private firms.

It was during this period that Matthew Boulton offered a solution to the problem by proposing that (1) each coin should contain its intrinsic value of metal, (2) a retaining collar should be used to maintain a constant diameter and (3) a broad raised rim should be used to save the coin from undue wear. He further proposed that a steam powered coinage press be used to produce a more uniformly finished coin with a greater rate of output.

In 1797 a remarkable series of full intrinsic value copper penny and twopenny pieces was issued. The twopence weighed two ounces and, being so large, these coins soon became known as "cartwheels." They were legal tender up to one shilling.

One unusual feature of this design is the inscription which is stamped incuse into a broad raised rim around each side of the coin. Dies were engraved by Conrad Heinrich Küchler, a talented Flemish die cutter. The coins were struck at the Soho Mint under the direction of Matthew Boulton.

A total of £6,018 worth of the twopence pieces was coined during 1797-1798. All of them were dated 1797. The cartwheels did not remain long in circulation owing to their inconvenient size. This is the only copper twopence in the British series. A small silver piece of this denomination is traditionally included in the Maundy series.

Diameter: 40.64mm; weight: 56.80 grams; composition: copper; edge: plain.

The "Cartwheel" Twopence of 1797

Date	Quantity Minted	Good	Fine	V. F.	Ex. F.	Unc.
1797	722,160	$4.00	$10.00	$20.00	$50.00	$100.00

SILVER TWOPENCE

Diameter: 13.44mm; weight: 0.94 grams; composition: .925 silver, .075 copper; edge: plain.

Silver halfgroats or twopences dated 1838, 1843 and 1848 were struck for Colonial use. They cannot be distinguished from the regular Maundy coins. One or two other years may have been struck for use in the colonies. See listing under Maundy coins, page 103.

SILVER THREEPENCES

A considerable quantity of threepences was struck for circulation beginning with the reign of William IV. They were from the same dies as the Maundy coins and thus it is not possible to distinguish between them. This situation existed with all of these struck for circulation until adoption of the three acorns reverse for threepences in 1927. The quantity minted includes both regular and Maundy coins. Dates are not listed in the section when coins were struck only for the Maundy sets.

Silver threepences are commonly called "thrup'nibits," in contrast to the brass pieces which were coined later and are known as "threepences."

William IV 1830-1837

These coins were issued for use only in the West Indies and not in England. Similar Maundy coins are dated 1831 through 1837. See page 102.

Diameter: 16.26mm; weight: 1.41 grams; composition: .925 silver, .075 copper; edge: plain.

Date	Quantity Minted	Good	Fine	V. F.	Ex. F.	Unc.
1834	401,016	$2.00	$4.00	$8.00	$17.50	$35.00
1835	491,040	2.00	4.00	8.00	17.50	35.00
1836	411,840	2.00	4.00	10.00	20.00	40.00
1837	42,768	2.00	5.00	12.50	25.00	50.00

Victoria 1837-1901.
Young Head

Coins of this series are indistinguishable from the Maundy pieces except that the Maundy coins usually look more like proofs and have a highly polished field. Approximately 4,000 of each of the threepences dated 1842, 1847, 1848, 1852 and 1869 were made for inclusion in the Maundy sets. It is possible that additional coins of these dates were issued for Colonial use; however, none has ever been positively identified as such.

Those dated 1838 to 1844 were issued for Colonial use only.

[47]

Silver Threepences

Young Head 1838-1887

Date	Quantity Minted	Good	Fine	V. Fine	Ex. Fine	Unc.	Proof
1838 . . . . } 1,203,840		$1.00	$3.00	$6.25	$16.00	$35.00	
1838 BRITANNIAB . /		15.00	25.00	70.00	100.00	150.00	
1839 570,240		2.00	5.00	10.00	25.00	50.00	
1840 633,600		1.25	3.50	6.50	17.50	40.00	
1841 443,520		1.25	3.50	6.50	17.50	42.00	
1843 2,027,520		1.00	3.25	6.00	15.00	32.50	
1844 1,045,400		1.25	3.50	7.00	20.00	45.00	
1845 1,314,720		1.00	3.00	6.00	14.00	30.00	
1846 47,520		1.25	3.50	7.00	20.00	45.00	
1849 126,720		1.25	3.50	7.00	20.00	50.00	
1850 950,400		1.00	3.25	6.25	16.00	35.00	
1851 479,065		1.00	3.25	6.25	16.00	35.00	
1853 31,680		1.50	4.00	8.00	22.00	45.00	
1854 1,467,246		1.00	3.25	6.25	16.00	35.00	
1855 383,350		1.50	4.00	8.00	22.00	45.00	
1856 1,013,760		1.00	3.00	6.00	14.00	30.00	
1857 1,758,240		1.25	3.50	7.00	20.00	40.00	
1858 1,441,440		1.00	3.00	6.00	14.00	30.00	
1859 3,579,840		1.00	3.00	6.00	14.00	30.00	
1860 3,405,600		1.00	3.00	6.00	15.00	32.50	
1861 3,294,720		1.00	3.00	6.00	15.00	32.50	
1862 1,156,320		1.00	3.00	6.50	17.50	37.50	
1863 950,400		1.25	3.50	7.00	20.00	45.00	
1864 1,330,560		1.00	3.00	6.00	15.00	32.50	
1865 1,742,400		1.25	3.50	7.00	21.00	45.00	
1866 1,900,800		.85	2.50	5.00	13.00	27.50	
1867 712,800		1.00	3.00	6.00	15.00	32.50	
1868 . . . . } 1,457,280		1.00	3.00	6.00	15.00	32.50	
1868 RRITANNIAR . . /		12.00	20.00	50.00	75.00	100.00	
1870 1,283,218		.85	2.50	5.00	13.00	27.50	
1871 999,633		1.00	3.00	6.00	14.00	30.00	
1872 1,293,271		.85	2.50	5.00	13.00	27.50	
1873 4,055,550		.65	1.75	3.50	8.50	19.00	
1874 4,427,031		.65	1.75	3.50	8.00	17.50	
1875 3,306,500		.65	1.75	3.50	8.00	17.50	
1876 1,834,389		.65	1.75	3.50	8.00	17.50	
1877 2,622,393		.65	1.75	3.50	8.00	17.50	
1878 2,419,975		.65	1.75	3.50	8.00	17.50	
1879 3,140,265		.65	1.75	3.50	8.00	17.50	$125.00
1880 1,610,069		.65	1.75	3.50	8.50	20.00	
1881 3,248,265		.65	1.75	3.50	8.00	17.50	
1882 472,965		1.25	3.50	7.00	20.00	40.00	
1883 4,369,971		.50	1.50	3.00	7.00	15.00	
1884 3,322,424		.50	1.50	3.00	7.00	16.00	
1885 5,183,653		.50	1.50	3.00	7.00	15.00	
1886 6,152,669		.50	1.50	3.00	7.00	15.00	
1887 young head . . . 2,780,761		.75	2.25	4.00	10.00	23.00	100.00

Jubilee Type 1887-1893

The Jubilee type threepence was struck in 1887 for currency but not until 1888 for inclusion in the Maundy sets. The rare threepence of 1893 differs from the Maundy threepence of that year because the coinage changed to the "Veiled Head" before Easter.

Date	Quantity Minted	Good	Fine	V. F.	Ex. F.	Unc.	Proof
1887 Jubilee........inc. above		$ .75	$1.75	$3.00	$6.00	$10.00	$50.00
1888.................518,199		1.00	2.25	5.00	10.00	18.00	
1889..............4,587,010		.75	1.75	3.00	6.00	10.00	
1890..............4,465,834		.75	1.75	3.00	6.00	10.00	
1891..............6,323,027		.75	1.75	3.00	6.00	10.00	
1892..............2,578,226		.75	1.75	3.50	7.00	12.00	
1893 open 3 in date	3,067,243	8.00	17.00	35.00	75.00	150.00	
1893 closed 3 in date		8.00	17.00	35.00	75.00	150.00	

Veiled Head 1893-1901

Date	Quantity Minted Proof	Regular	Good	Fine	V. F.	Ex. F.	Unc.	Proof
1893..(1,312)		inc. above	.35	.75	2.25	5.50	9.00	80.00
1894..........1,608,603			.60	1.00	3.00	7.00	12.00	
1895..........4,788,609			.60	1.00	3.00	7.00	12.00	
1896..........4,598,442			.45	.80	2.50	6.00	10.00	
1897..........4,541,294			.35	.75	2.25	5.50	9.00	
1898..........4,567,177			.35	.75	2.25	5.50	9.00	
1899..........6,246,281			.35	.75	2.00	5.00	8.00	
1900.........10,644,480			.35	.75	2.00	5.00	8.00	
1901..........6,098,400			.35	.75	2.00	5.00	8.00	

Edward VII 1901-1910

The portrait on the threepence corresponds with the other denominations in this series. The reverse is the same as was used on the Victorian coins. A slight change was made in the style of the figure three during 1904. Coins dated 1902-1904 show a large ball on the end of the denomination 3 nearly touching the center diagonal line. Coins made in the late part of 1904 to the end of the reign have a more modern looking figure three with a smaller ball.

Silver Threepences

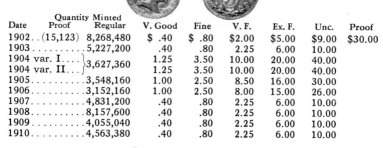

Date	Quantity Minted Proof	Quantity Minted Regular	V. Good	Fine	V. F.	Ex. F.	Unc.	Proof
1902..	(15,123)	8,268,480	$ .40	$ .80	$2.00	$5.00	$9.00	$30.00
1903		5,227,200	.40	.80	2.25	6.00	10.00	
1904 var. I....		3,627,360	1.25	3.50	10.00	20.00	40.00	
1904 var. II...			1.25	3.50	10.00	20.00	40.00	
1905		3,548,160	1.00	2.50	8.50	16.00	30.00	
1906		3,152,160	1.00	2.50	8.00	15.00	26.00	
1907		4,831,200	.40	.80	2.25	6.00	10.00	
1908		8,157,600	.40	.80	2.25	6.00	10.00	
1909		4,055,040	.40	.80	2.25	6.00	10.00	
1910		4,563,380	.40	.80	2.25	6.00	10.00	

George V 1910-1936

The first head is similar to the other early coins of this reign. The reverse continues unchanged until 1927. These early threepences are exactly like the Maundy coins. Those dated 1923 and 1924 were made only for sets.

During 1920 the metal content was changed to 50% silver. This change, however, did not occur in the Maundy coins until the following year.

Diameter: 16.26mm; weight: 1.41 grams; composition: *before 1920*, .925 silver, .075 copper; *1920*, .500 silver, .400 copper, .100 nickel; *1921*, .500 silver, .450 copper, .050 manganese; *1922-1926*, .500 silver, .500 copper; edge: plain.

Date		Quantity	V. Good	Fine	V. F.	Unc.	Proof
1911...	(6,007)	5,841,084	.50	1.50	3.50	7.00	40.00
1912		8,932,825	.50	1.50	3.50	7.00	
1913		7,143,242	.50	1.50	3.50	7.00	
1914		6,733,584	.50	2.00	3.50	7.00	
1915		5,450,617	.75	2.00	4.00	9.00	
1916		18,555,201	.30	1.00	2.00	5.00	
1917		21,662,490	.30	1.00	2.00	5.00	
1918		20,630,909	.30	1.00	2.00	5.00	
1919		16,845,687	.30	1.00	2.00	5.00	
1920 .925 fine		16,703,597	.30	1.00	2.00	5.00	
1920 .500 fine			.40	1.25	3.00	6.00	
1921		8,749,301	.40	1.25	3.00	6.00	
1922		7,979,998	.50	1.50	3.50	7.00	
1925		3,731,859	1.25	3.50	8.00	15.00	
1926		4,107,910	2.00	6.00	12.00	20.00	
1926 modified effigy....			2.00	7.00	15.00	22.00	

The smaller, modified effigy was introduced during 1926. The corresponding change was not made in the Maundy coins until 1928, after a new reverse design had been adopted for the regular threepence. This new reverse depicts three oak-sprigs with three acorns and a small G in the center. Mintage figures are for regular coins only and do not include the Maundy pieces.

Diameter: 16.26mm; weight: 1.41 grams; composition: .500 silver, .400 copper, .050 nickel, .050 zinc; edge: plain.

Date	Quantity Minted Proof	Regular	V. Good	Fine	V. F.	Ex. F.	Unc.	Proof
1927 . (15,022)	Proof only							$60.00
1928	1,302,106		$1.00	$2.50	$6.00	$12.00	$20.00	
1930	1,319,412		.80	1.50	5.00	10.00	15.00	
1931	6,251,936			.30	1.00	2.00	5.00	
1932	5,887,325			.30	.75	1.50	4.00	
1933	5,578,541			.30	.75	1.50	4.00	
1934	7,405,954			.30	.75	1.50	4.00	
1935	7,027,654			.30	.75	1.50	4.00	

Edward VIII 1936

Silver threepences dated 1936 were issued during the reign of Edward VIII. All of these coins have the name and portrait of George V due to the fact that King Edward abdicated before new dies were used. See section on the brass threepence (page 52) for additional information.

1936	3,238,670			.30	.75	1.50	4.00	

George VI 1937-1952

The new design for the reverse of the silver threepence consists of the shield of St. George on a Tudor rose dividing the date. The designer's initials KG, Kruger Gray, are below.

Both the silver threepence coins and the twelve-sided nickel-brass pieces were coined from 1937 to 1946. The silver coinage was discontinued in 1946. All of the silver threepence pieces minted in 1946 were dated 1945. These were never issued and were later melted at the mint. Only a single specimen is reported to exist.

Coins dated 1942 through 1944 were struck in small quantities for use solely in the West Indies. 1,063,624 pieces were minted in 1944, and an additional 941,929 were minted in 1945 — all from dies dated 1944. Many of the 1944 coins and the entire 1945 issue were supposedly melted by the mint.

Date	Proof	Regular	V. Good	Fine	V. F.	Ex. F.	Unc.	Proof
1937 . . (26,402)		8,148,156		.25	.50	1.25	3.00	12.00
1938		6,402,473		.25	.50	1.25	3.00	
1939		1,355,860		.40	1.25	4.00	7.00	
1940		7,914,401		.30	.75	1.50	4.00	
1941		7,979,411		.30	.75	1.50	4.00	
1942		4,144,051	1.00	2.00	5.00	12.00	20.00	
1943		1,379,220	1.00	2.50	6.00	15.00	25.00	
1944		2,005,553	2.00	4.50	10.00	22.00	35.00	
1945		371,600	Entire issue supposedly melted by the mint.					

NICKEL-BRASS THREEPENCES
Edward VIII 1936

No coins bearing the portrait of Edward VIII were issued for circulation. Dies, however, were prepared for the anticipated coinage and a few specimens were struck. A new type threepence was proposed and dies for a nickel-brass twelve-sided coin were designed by T. H. Paget, obverse, and Miss Madge Kitchener, reverse. A few specimens, all dated 1937, somehow reached circulation. Normal and thin varieties of this coinage have been reported. They are all extremely rare. A second type is known with this obverse and the regular reverse of 1937.

The portrait is shown facing to the left as on the coins of George V. This break with the tradition of each monarch facing in the opposite direction was at the King's own request. This circumstance was somewhat rectified by the coins of George VI which also show the King's head facing left.

1937 Exceedingly rare...

George VI 1937-1952

The nickel-brass threepence was introduced into the coinage of George VI despite the fact that the silver threepence was also coined, simultaneously, until 1946. The new type became popular immediately because of its convenient size. The reverse design, that of a thrift plant, is an adaptation of the design intended for use on the threepence of Edward VIII.

In 1949 the legend was changed to eliminate IND:IMP:. Proofs were struck every year and all are very rare with the exception of those issued in specimen sets for the years 1937, 1950 and 1951.

The angles of the edges on these coins were rounded in 1941 and throughout the war years to speed up production. The sharp edges were returned in 1950.

Diameter: 21.10mm across flats, 21.90mm across corners; weight: 6.80 grams; composition: .790 copper, .010 nickel, .200 zinc; edge: plain, dodecagonal (12-sided).

1937-1948   *1949-1952*

Date	Quantity Minted Proof	Regular	V. F.	Ex. F.	Unc.	Proof
1937	(26,402)	45,707,957	$ .25	$ .75	$2.50	$12.00
1938		14,532,332	1.00	4.50	10.00	

Date	Quantity Minted Proof	Regular	V. F.	Ex. F.	Unc.	Proof
1939		5,603,021	$1.50	$6.50	$15.00	
1940		12,636,018	.85	3.25	7.50	
1941		60,239,489	.35	1.25	4.00	
1942		103,214,400	.35	1.25	3.50	
1943		101,702,400	.35	1.25	3.50	
1944		69,760,000	.35	1.25	3.50	
1945		33,942,466	.50	2.00	6.00	
1946		620,734	8.00	60.00	150.00	
1948		4,230,400	2.00	10.00	20.00	
1949		464,000	12.00	80.00	200.00	
1950	(17,513)	1,600,000	2.00	12.00	30.00	$35.00
1951	(20,000)	1,184,000	3.50	15.00	35.00	35.00
1952		25,494,400	.40	1.50	4.00	

Elizabeth II 1952-

The portrait of Elizabeth II was designed by Mrs. Mary Gillick. The early dies of 1953 were not satisfactory and were recut during the year to produce a more pleasing effigy. The reverse was designed by William Gardner and depicts an ancient portcullis, a prototype of which was first used on coins of Elizabeth I. In 1954 the portrait was further retouched and the legend altered to eliminate BRITT:OMN:. Proofs exist for every date and all are very rare with the exception of 1953 and 1970 coins which were issued in specimen sets.

1953   *1954-1970*

1953	(40,000)	30,618,000	.25	1.00	3.25	8.00
1954		41,720,000	.35	1.25	4.50	
1955		41,075,200	.35	1.25	4.50	
1956		36,801,600	.35	1.25	4.50	
1957		24,294,400	.35	1.25	4.00	
1958		20,504,000	1.00	3.50	9.00	
1959		28,499,200	.35	1.25	3.50	
1960		83,078,400	.25	.75	5.00	
1961		41,102,400		.35	1.00	
1962		51,545,600		.35	1.00	
1963		35,280,000		.20	.50	
1964		44,867,200		.20	.50	
1965		27,160,000		.20	.50	
1966		53,760,000		.15	.50	
1967		93,060,800		.15	.50	
1970 issued only in sets						2.00

SILVER SIXPENCES
George III 1760-1820

Sixpences of George III were issued in 1787 of two different kinds. The listing in this catalogue, however, properly begins with the last or "new" coinage designed by Pistrucci and introduced in 1816. It has as its design a garnished shield, crowned, within a Garter.

Diameter: 19.41mm; weight: 2.83 grams; composition: .925 silver, .075 copper; edge: reeded.

Date	Quantity Minted	Good	Fine	V. Fine	Ex. Fine	Unc.	Proof
1816............	} 10,921,680	$1.25	$2.00	$5.00	$12.00	$28.00	
1817............		1.25	2.00	5.00	14.00	30.00	$90.00
1818............	4,284,720	2.00	3.00	7.00	20.00	50.00	100.00
1819 9 over 8........							150.00
1819............	4,712,400	1.50	2.50	6.00	15.00	35.00	100.00
1820............	} 1,488,960	1.50	2.50	6.00	15.00	35.00	100.00
1820 inverted 1 in date........		2.50	4.00	9.00	20.00	50.00	

George IV 1820-1830

The first coins of George IV show a laureate head facing left and are the work of Benedetto Pistrucci. The reverse shows an ornate crowned shield surrounded by thistle, rose and shamrock. The second type has a square-topped shield, crowned, surrounded by the Garter. In 1826 a new head was designed, at the King's request, by William Wyon. The reverse shows a lion on a crown.

An unusual variety of the 1821 sixpence originally read BITANNIAR. This was changed in the die to BBITANNIAR with faint traces of the second B altered to look like an R. The extremely rare pieces dated 1820 are patterns.

First Reverse 1821

1821............	} 863,280	3.00	5.00	12.00	35.00	60.00	80.00
1821 BBITANNIAR.....		7.00	15.00	25.00	60.00	150.00	

Second Reverse 1824-1826

Date	Quantity Minted	Good	Fine	V. F.	Ex. F.	Unc.	Proof
1824	633,600	$3.00	$5.00	$12.00	$30.00	$55.00	$100.00
1825	483,120	3.00	5.00	12.00	30.00	55.00	100.00
1826	689,040	7.00	15.00	30.00	75.00	150.00	175.00

When the King's portrait was changed, Pistrucci was commissioned to engrave the obverse dies from a bust by Sir Francis Chantrey. When he refused to copy the work of another artist, the task was given to W. Wyon who produced his fine "bare head."

1826	inc. above	2.00	3.00	10.00	27.50	50.00	100.00
1827	166,320	5.00	10.00	25.00	50.00	100.00	
1828	15,840	3.50	6.00	15.00	32.00	60.00	
1829	403,920	2.00	3.00	10.00	30.00	50.00	200.00

William IV 1830-1837

The proof coins of 1834, 1835 and 1836 all have a round top 3 in the date. All other coins have the normal 3 with straight top.

1831	1,340,195	3.00	5.00	12.00	30.00	50.00	150.00
1834	5,892,480	2.00	4.00	10.00	27.50	50.00	225.00
1835	1,552,320	3.00	5.00	16.00	35.00	60.00	500.00
1836	1,987,920	6.00	14.00	30.00	70.00	125.00	500.00
1837	506,880	3.00	5.00	12.00	32.00	55.00	500.00

Silver Sixpences

Victoria 1837-1901

There are three distinguishable varieties of the first, or young head of Victoria used on the sixpence. The changes were made in 1867 and 1880. Sixpences dated 1864 through 1879 usually have a small die number just above the date. This number served as an identification and was changed on each new die.

Approximately 10,000 pieces of the 1878 DRITANNIAR variety were released into circulation in Cyprus. All have reverse die number 6.

First Young Head

Diameter: 19.41mm; weight: 2.83 grams; composition: .925 silver, .075 copper; edge: reeded.

First Young Head   Die number position.

Date	Quantity Minted	Good	Fine	V. Fine	Ex. Fine	Unc.	Proof
1838	1,607,760	$1.25	$3.00	$7.00	$25.00	$40.00	$140.00
1839	3,310,560	1.25	3.00	7.00	25.00	40.00	125.00
1840	2,098,800	1.50	4.50	11.00	32.00	55.00	
1841	1,386,000	1.50	4.00	10.00	30.00	50.00	
1842	601,920	1.50	4.00	10.00	30.00	55.00	
1843	3,160,080	1.25	3.50	8.00	25.00	40.00	
1844 nor. date. ⎫	⎧	1.25	3.50	8.00	25.00	40.00	
1844 lg. 44.... ⎭	3,975,840	2.00	5.00	10.00	30.00	50.00	
1845	3,714,480	1.25	3.50	8.00	25.00	42.00	
1846	4,268,880	1.25	3.50	8.00	25.00	40.00	
1847 A single specimen of this date has been reported.							
1848 8 over 6 ... ⎫		7.00	15.00	35.00	70.00	150.00	
1848 8 over 7 ... ⎬ 586,080		8.00	17.50	37.50	75.00	150.00	
1848 .... ⎭		6.00	12.00	27.50	60.00	100.00	
1849	205,920	Unknown.					
1850 .... ⎫		1.50	4.00	11.00	30.00	55.00	
1850 5 over 3 ... ⎭ 498,960		7.00	15.00	35.00	70.00	150.00	
1851	2,288,107	1.50	4.00	12.50	35.00	60.00	
1852	904,586	1.25	3.50	9.00	30.00	50.00	
1853	3,837,930	1.25	3.25	8.00	25.00	37.50	125.00
1854	840,116	15.00	30.00	100.00	200.00	300.00	
1855	1,129,084	1.25	3.25	8.00	25.00	37.50	200.00
1856	2,779,920	1.25	3.25	8.00	25.00	37.50	

Normal Date   Large 44   1848 – 8 over 7

Date	Quantity Minted	Good	Fine	V. F.	Ex. F.	Unc.	Proof
1857	2,233,440	$1.25	$3.75	$10.00	$27.50	$47.50	
1858	1,932,480	1.25	3.50	9.00	25.00	45.00	$225.00
1859 9 over 8	4,688,640	7.00	15.00	35.00	70.00	110.00	
1859		1.25	3.00	7.00	20.00	35.00	
1860	1,100,880	1.25	3.75	10.00	30.00	55.00	
1861	601,920	Unknown.					
1862	990,000	6.00	12.00	27.50	60.00	100.00	
1863	491,040	6.00	12.00	27.50	60.00	100.00	
1864	4,253,040	1.25	3.25	8.00	22.00	40.00	
1865	1,631,520	1.50	4.00	10.00	30.00	50.00	
1866	5,140,080	2.00	5.00	12.00	35.00	60.00	
1866 no number		7.00	15.00	35.00	70.00	120.00	

Second Young Head

Date	Quantity Minted	Good	Fine	V. F.	Ex. F.	Unc.	Proof
1867	1,362,240	2.50	6.00	13.00	37.50	70.00	175.00
1868	1,069,200	2.50	6.00	13.00	37.50	70.00	
1869	388,080	2.50	6.00	13.00	37.50	70.00	
1870	479,613	3.00	7.00	15.00	40.00	75.00	175.00
1871	3,662,684	1.25	3.00	7.00	20.00	35.00	175.00
1871 no number		2.00	5.00	12.00	35.00	65.00	
1872	3,382,048	1.25	3.00	7.00	20.00	32.00	
1873	4,594,733	1.00	2.50	6.00	17.50	28.00	
1874	4,225,726	1.00	2.50	6.00	17.50	28.00	
1875	3,256,545	1.00	2.50	6.00	17.50	28.00	
1876	841,435	2.50	6.00	13.00	37.50	70.00	
1877	4,066,486	1.00	2.50	6.00	17.50	28.00	
1877 no number		1.25	3.00	7.00	20.00	35.00	
1878 8 over 7	2,624,525	10.00	20.00	100.00	150.00	200.00	
1878		1.25	3.00	6.00	17.50	28.00	175.00
1878 DRITANNIAR		12.00	25.00	110.00	150.00	200.00	
1879	3,326,313	2.50	6.00	13.00	37.50	70.00	
1879 no number		1.00	2.25	6.00	17.50	28.00	
1880 second young head		1.25	3.00	7.00	20.00	35.00	

Third Young Head

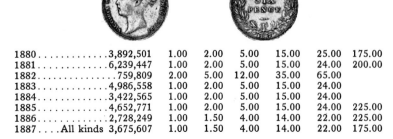

Date	Quantity Minted	Good	Fine	V. F.	Ex. F.	Unc.	Proof
1880	3,892,501	1.00	2.00	5.00	15.00	25.00	175.00
1881	6,239,447	1.00	2.00	5.00	15.00	24.00	200.00
1882	759,809	2.00	5.00	12.00	35.00	65.00	
1883	4,986,558	1.00	2.00	5.00	15.00	24.00	
1884	3,422,565	1.00	2.00	5.00	15.00	24.00	
1885	4,652,771	1.00	2.00	5.00	15.00	24.00	225.00
1886	2,728,249	1.00	1.50	4.00	14.00	22.00	225.00
1887 All kinds	3,675,607	1.00	1.50	4.00	14.00	22.00	175.00

Silver Sixpences

Victoria — *Jubilee Head*

In 1887 a new type coinage was issued to celebrate the Queen's golden jubilee. The first design used on the reverse of the sixpence was found unsatisfactory because of its resemblance to the half sovereign and was changed late in the year to the familiar crowned SIX PENCE.

"Withdrawn" Jubilee Type 1887

Date	Quantity Minted Proof	Quantity Minted Regular	Good	Fine	V. F.	Ex. F.	Unc.	Proof
1887 Withdrawn type								
All kinds. .3,675,607			$ .75	$1.25	$2.50	$4.50	$8.00	$50.00

Second Jubilee Type 1887-1893

		Good	Fine	V. F.	Ex. F.	Unc.	Proof
1887 Crowned SIX PENCE							
All kinds. .3,675,607		.60	1.00	2.00	5.00	10.00	100.00
1888. 4,197,698		.75	1.25	3.00	6.50	12.00	
1889. 8,738,928		.75	1.25	3.00	6.50	12.00	
1890. 9,386,955		.90	1.50	4.00	8.00	14.00	
1891. 7,022,734		.90	1.50	4.00	8.00	14.00	
1892. 6,245,746		.90	1.50	4.00	8.00	14.00	
1893. 7,350,619		50.00	125.00	250.00	500.00	800.00	

Victoria
Veiled Head

		Good	Fine	V. F.	Ex. F.	Unc.	Proof
1893. .(1,312) inc. above		.75	1.25	3.00	8.00	14.00	40.00
1894. 3,467,704		.90	1.50	4.50	10.00	16.00	
1895. 7,024,631		.90	1.50	4.50	10.00	16.00	
1896. 6,651,699		.90	1.50	4.50	10.00	16.00	
1897. 5,031,498		.75	1.25	3.00	8.00	14.00	
1898. 5,914,100		.75	1.25	3.00	8.00	14.00	
1899. 7,996,804		.75	1.25	3.00	8.00	14.00	
1900. 8,984,354		.60	1.00	2.50	7.00	14.00	
1901. 5,108,757		.60	1.00	2.50	6.50	12.00	

Edward VII 1901-1910

The proof coins issued in the specimen sets of 1902 all have a dull matte surface.

Date	Quantity Minted Proof	Regular	Fine	V. F.	Ex. F.	Unc.	Proof
1902	(15,123)	6,367,378	$1.50	$4.00	$10.00	$16.00	$30.00
1903		5,410,096	2.00	6.00	18.00	35.00	
1904		4,487,098	3.00	10.00	30.00	45.00	
1905		4,235,556	2.50	8.00	25.00	40.00	
1906		7,641,146	1.75	5.00	14.00	25.00	
1907		8,733,673	2.00	6.00	15.00	30.00	
1908		6,739,491	2.75	9.00	30.00	45.00	
1909		6,584,017	2.00	6.00	16.00	35.00	
1910		12,490,724	1.50	4.00	12.00	20.00	

George V 1910-1936

Several changes were made in the sixpence coinage of George V. The first reverse depicts a lion on a crown dividing the date. In 1920 the metal content was lowered to 50 percent silver and 50 percent alloy. Coins of both the old and the new alloy were issued in 1920. During 1926 the effigy was modified and made slightly smaller to correspond with the other denominations. The new reverse type was first introduced in the proof sets of 1927. The design incorporates three oak sprigs with six acorns. Coins made in 1931 and after have closer reeding on the edge.

Variety I – 1911-1926

1911	(6,007)	9,155,310	1.00	2.00	6.00	12.00	35.00
1912		10,984,129	1.25	3.00	8.00	20.00	
1913		7,499,833	1.50	3.50	10.00	25.00	
1914		22,714,602	1.00	1.50	5.00	10.00	
1915		15,694,597	1.00	1.50	5.00	10.00	
1916		22,207,178	1.00	1.50	5.00	10.00	
1917		7,725,475	1.25	2.50	7.00	18.00	
1918		27,558,743	1.00	1.50	5.00	10.00	
1919		13,375,447	1.00	2.00	6.00	12.00	
1920 .925 fine		14,136,287	1.00	2.00	6.50	15.00	

Silver Sixpences

Diameter: 19.41mm; weight: 2.83 grams; composition: *before 1920*, .925 silver, .075 copper; *1920*, .500 silver, .400 copper, .100 nickel; *1921*, .500 silver, .450 copper, .050 manganese; *1922-1926*, .500 silver, .500 copper; edge: reeded.

Variety II – 1926-1927

	Quantity Minted					
Date	Proof	Regular	V. Fine	Ex. Fine	Unc.	Proof
1920 .500 fine		incl. above	$2.00	$6.50	$15.00	
1921		30,339,741	1.50	6.00	12.00	
1922		16,878,890	1.50	6.00	12.00	
1923		6,382,793	4.00	12.00	27.50	
1924		17,444,218	1.50	6.00	12.00	
1925		12,720,558	1.50	6.50	15.00	
1925 broad rim			1.50	6.00	12.00	
1926 variety I		21,809,621	1.50	6.50	15.00	
1926 variety II			1.25	5.00	10.00	
1927		68,939,873	1.25	5.00	11.00	

Diameter: 19.41mm; weight: 2.83 grams; composition: .500 silver, .400 copper, .050 nickel, .050 zinc; edge: reeded.

1927	(15,000)	Proof only				$20.00
1928		23,123,384	.75	3.00	6.00	
1929		28,319,326	.75	3.00	7.00	
1930		16,990,289	1.25	5.00	10.00	
1931		16,873,268	1.25	6.00	12.00	
1932		9,406,117	1.50	7.00	14.00	
1933		22,185,083	1.25	5.00	10.00	
1934		9,304,009	1.50	7.00	14.00	
1935		13,995,621	.75	3.00	7.00	

Edward VIII 1936

Sixpences dated 1936 were issued during the reign of Edward VIII. All of these coins have the name and portrait of George V due to the fact that King Edward abdicated before the new type was used.

| 1936 | | 24,380,171 | .60 | 2.50 | 5.00 | |

George VI 1936-1952

The new design on the sixpence was the work of Kruger Gray; it features a crowned **GRI** monogram, dividing the date. In 1947 the metal was changed to an alloy of 75 percent copper and 25 percent nickel. Coins of this new alloy have closer reeding on the edge.

Diameter: 19.41mm; weight: 2.83 grams; composition: .500 silver, .400 copper, .050 nickel, .050 zinc; edge: reeded.

Date	Quantity Minted Proof	Quantity Minted Regular	V. F.	Ex. F.	Unc.	Proof
1937	(26,402)	22,302,524	$ .50	$1.50	$3.00	$12.00
1938		13,402,701	1.25	3.50	10.00	
1939		28,670,304	.50	1.50	4.50	
1940		20,875,196	.75	2.00	6.00	
1941		23,086,616	.75	2.00	6.00	
1942		44,942,785	.50	1.00	2.50	
1943		46,927,111	.50	1.00	2.25	
1944		37,952,600	.50	1.00	2.25	
1945		39,939,259	.50	1.00	2.25	
1946		43,466,407	.50	1.00	2.25	

Copper-Nickel

Diameter: 19.41mm; weight: 2.83 grams; composition: .750 copper, .250 nickel; edge: reeded.

Date	Regular	V. F.	Ex. F.	Unc.
1947	29,993,263	.50	1.00	3.00
1948	88,323,540	.50	1.00	2.25

A major change was made in 1949 when the legend was altered to eliminate IND IMP from the title and monogram changed to **GR VI**.

The 1952 issue was struck for use in the West Indies.

Date	Proof	Regular	V. F.	Ex. F.	Unc.	Proof
1949		41,355,515	.30	1.00	3.00	
1950	(17,513)	32,741,955	.30	1.00	4.00	10.00
1951	(20,000)	40,399,491	.30	1.00	3.50	10.00
1952		1,013,477	3.50	12.00	37.50	

COPPER-NICKEL SIXPENCES
Elizabeth II 1952-

The portrait of Elizabeth II was designed by Mrs. Mary Gillick. The early dies of 1953 were not satisfactory and were recut during the year to produce a sharper, more detailed portrait. The reverse was designed by F. G. Fuller and modeled by Cecil Thomas; it has a garland of interlaced rose, thistle, shamrock and leek.

Diameter: 19.41mm; weight: 2.83 grams; composition: .750 copper, .250 nickel; edge: reeded.

1953

Date	Quantity Minted Proof	Quantity Minted Regular	Ex. F.	Unc.	Proof
1953	(40,000)	70,323,876	$ .50	$1.50	$7.00

BRITT: OMN: Omitted

The obverse legend was altered in 1954 to eliminate BRITT: OMN: from the Royal Title. Proof coins dated 1970 were made for collector's sets.

1954-1970

1954	105,241,150	.75	3.50	
1955	109,929,554	.35	1.50	
1956	109,841,555	.35	1.50	
1957	105,654,290	.30	1.00	
1958	123,518,527	.75	3.50	
1959	93,089,441	.25	.60	
1960	103,288,346	.75	3.50	
1961	115,052,017	.30	1.25	
1962	178,359,637		.60	
1963	112,964,000		.50	
1964	152,336,000		.50	
1965	129,644,000		.50	
1966	175,676,000		.35	
1967	148,544,000		.35	
1970 issued only in sets				2.00

SILVER SHILLINGS
George III 1760-1820

A small issue of £100 worth of shillings dated 1763 was struck for distribution when the Earl of Northumberland entered Dublin as Lord Lieutenant. These are popularly known as "Northumberland" shillings.

In 1787 a great quantity of shillings was issued for general circulation and these are still relatively common today. The small issue of shillings coined in 1798 are known as the "Dorrien and Magens" shillings because they were made from silver bullion sent to the Mint for coinage by the firm of Dorrien, Magens, Mello, Martin and Harrison. The shillings of 1786 are proofs or patterns only. The listing in this catalogue begins with the last or "new" coinage of 1816 to 1820. Dies are by Pistrucci and T. Wyon, Jr.

Diameter: 23.60mm; weight: 5.66 grams; composition: .925 silver, .075 copper; edge: reeded.

Date	Quantity Minted	Good	Fine	V. Fine	Ex. Fine	Unc.	Proof
1816		$1.50	$3.50	$8.00	$20.00	$40.00	$175.00
1817 GEOE (error)	23,031,360	20.00	50.00	100.00	250.00		
1817		1.50	3.50	8.00	20.00	40.00	175.00
1818	1,342,440	2.50	5.00	12.00	30.00	75.00	
1819 9 over 8	7,595,280	4.00	8.00	20.00	60.00	120.00	
1819		1.50	4.00	10.00	22.00	45.00	
1820	7,975,440	1.50	4.00	10.00	22.00	45.00	

George IV 1820-1830

The obverse showing the King's laureate head is the work of Pistrucci. It was used on the first and second issues. The reverse is by his assistant, J. B. Merlen. When the King's portrait was changed in 1825, Pistrucci was commissioned to copy a bust by Sir Francis Chantrey, but when he refused to do this, the task was given to W. Wyon, who produced the fine "bare head."

1821

1821	2,463,120	3.00	7.00	20.00	50.00	90.00	200.00

Silver Shillings

1823-1825

Date	Quantity Minted	Good	Fine	V. F.	Ex. F.	Unc.	Proof
1823............693,000		$5.00	$10.00	$30.00	$75.00	$130.00	$250.00
1824..........4,158,000		2.50	5.00	15.00	40.00	80.00	225.00
1825 5 over 3. ⎫ 2,459,160		4.00	8.00	20.00	50.00	100.00	
1825.........⎭		3.00	6.00	17.50	45.00	90.00	225.00

1825.........incl. above		2.00	5.00	10.00	35.00	60.00	150.00
1826 6 over 2. ⎫ 6,351,840		4.00	8.00	20.00	50.00	100.00	
1826.........⎭		2.00	5.00	10.00	35.00	60.00	150.00
1827............574,200		3.00	7.00	25.00	60.00	120.00	
1829............879,120		2.50	6.00	15.00	45.00	90.00	175.00

William IV 1830-1837

Only one type of shilling was issued during the short reign of William IV. The portrait was engraved by William Wyon from a model by Chantrey. The reverse design is by Merlen. Some of the proof specimens have the normal straight top three in the date while others have a round top three.

1831.........Proof only							200.00
1834..........3,223,440		2.50	6.50	16.00	40.00	75.00	350.00
1835..........1,449,360		3.00	8.00	20.00	50.00	100.00	350.00
1836..........3,567,960		2.50	6.50	16.00	40.00	75.00	400.00
1837............479,160		3.00	8.00	20.00	50.00	100.00	350.00

Victoria 1837-1901

The young head shilling of Victoria was designed by W. Wyon. The reverse is by Merlen and the same as that used on the preceding issue. During the fifty years that these shillings were coined, several changes were made in an effort to show the Queen's portrait with aging features. Those coined in 1838 and part of 1839 show the designer's initials, WW, on the truncation.

From 1864 to 1879 most of these coins show a small die number above the date. This number apparently started with number one each year and sometimes exceeded 150.

Diameter: 23.60mm; weight: 5.66 grams; composition: .925 silver, .075 copper; edge: reeded.

Young Head

Date	Quantity Minted	Good	Fine	V. Fine	Ex. F.	Unc.	Proof
1838 1,956,240		$2.50	$5.00	$15.00	$35.00	$60.00	$200.00
1839 with ww .	\	2.50	5.00	15.00	35.00	60.00	200.00
1839 w/o ww .	} 5,666,760	2.00	4.00	12.00	30.00	50.00	
1840 1,639,440		5.00	12.00	30.00	90.00	125.00	200.00
1841 875,160		3.50	7.00	18.00	50.00	75.00	
1842 2,094,840		2.00	4.00	12.00	30.00	50.00	
1843 1,465,200		3.50	7.00	18.00	50.00	80.00	300.00
1844 4,466,880		2.00	4.00	12.00	30.00	50.00	
1845 4,082,760		3.50	7.00	18.00	50.00	80.00	
1846 4,031,280		1.50	3.50	10.00	25.00	40.00	
1848 8 over 6 . . 1,041,480		7.00	15.00	40.00	110.00	150.00	
1849 645,480		2.00	4.00	12.00	30.00	50.00	
1850 . . . . \	} 685,080	25.00	100.00	200.00	400.00	700.00	
1850 50 over 46 . /		30.00	125.00	250.00	500.00	800.00	
1851 470,071		5.00	12.00	35.00	100.00	150.00	250.00
1852 1,306,574		1.50	3.50	10.00	25.00	40.00	
1853 4,256,188		1.50	3.50	10.00	25.00	40.00	250.00
1854 552,414		15.00	40.00	100.00	250.00	400.00	
1855 1,368,499		1.50	3.50	10.00	25.00	40.00	
1856 3,168,000		1.50	3.50	10.00	25.00	40.00	
1857 REG F: Ɔ: \	} 2,562,120	10.00	20.00	50.00	150.00		
1857 . . . . /		1.50	3.50	10.00	25.00	40.00	
1858 3,108,600		1.50	3.50	10.00	25.00	40.00	
1859 4,561,920		1.50	3.50	10.00	25.00	40.00	
1860 1,671,120		3.50	7.00	18.00	50.00	75.00	
1861 1,382,040		3.50	7.00	18.00	50.00	75.00	
1862 954,360		5.00	12.00	30.00	90.00	125.00	
1863 859,320		5.00	12.00	30.00	90.00	125.00	
1864 4,518,360		1.50	3.50	10.00	25.00	40.00	
1865 5,619,240		1.50	3.50	10.00	25.00	40.00	
1866 4,989,600		1.50	3.50	10.00	25.00	40.00	
1866 BBITANNIAR		7.00	15.00	40.00	100.00	150.00	

Silver Shillings

Date	Quantity Minted Proof	Regular	Good	Fine	V. F.	Ex.F.	Unc.	Proof
1867		2,166,120	$2.50	$5.00	$15.00	$35.00	$60.00	$300.00
1868		3,330,360	1.25	3.00	8.00	20.00	35.00	
1869		736,560	2.50	5.00	15.00	40.00	75.00	
1870		1,467,471	2.00	4.00	12.00	30.00	50.00	
1871		4,910,010	1.10	2.50	7.00	18.00	30.00	300.00
1872		8,897,781	1.10	2.50	7.00	18.00	30.00	
1873		6,489,598	1.00	2.00	5.00	15.00	25.00	
1874		5,503,747	1.10	2.50	7.00	18.00	30.00	
1875		4,353,983	1.10	2.50	7.00	18.00	30.00	
1876		1,057,487	1.50	3.50	10.00	25.00	40.00	
1877		2,980,703	1.10	2.50	7.00	18.00	30.00	
1878		3,127,131	1.10	2.50	7.00	18.00	30.00	300.00
1879		3,611,507	2.00	4.00	12.00	30.00	50.00	300.00
1880		4,842,786	1.00	2.00	5.00	15.00	25.00	300.00
1881		5,255,332	1.00	2.00	5.00	15.00	25.00	300.00
1882		1,611,786	2.50	5.00	15.00	40.00	75.00	
1883		7,281,450	1.00	2.00	5.00	15.00	25.00	
1884		3,923,993	1.00	2.00	5.00	15.00	25.00	300.00
1885		3,336,527	1.00	2.00	5.00	15.00	25.00	300.00
1886		2,086,819	1.00	2.25	6.00	17.00	27.50	325.00
1887		4,034,133	1.25	3.00	8.00	20.00	35.00	325.00

Victoria — Jubilee Head

In 1887 the design on the English coinage was changed to celebrate the golden jubilee of the Queen's reign. A total of 4,034,133 shillings was issued in 1887. These included both the "young head" coins and the "jubilee head" coins. The first issue of the jubilee shilling shows a rather small head which was modified in 1889 and replaced with a larger, more attractive effigy. Sir J. Boehm designed both styles of the jubilee shillings. The small head and the large head varieties were both issued in 1889.

Small Jubilee Head 1887-1889   Large Jubilee Head 1889-1892

Date	Quantity	Good	Fine	V. F.	Ex.F.	Unc.	Proof
1887..(1,084) inc. above		.75	1.25	2.00	4.00	8.00	50.00
1888*	4,526,856	.75	1.50	3.50	12.00	16.00	
1889 sm. head.	7,039,628	8.00	18.00	45.00	140.00	220.00	
1889 lg. head..		1.00	2.00	5.00	14.00	18.00	400.00
1890	8,794,042	1.00	2.00	5.00	14.00	18.00	
1891	5,665,348	1.00	2.50	6.00	15.00	20.00	450.00
1892	4,591,622	1.00	2.50	6.00	16.00	22.00	

*Traces of a 7 can be seen under the final 8 on some of these pieces.

Victoria — Veiled Head

The obverse of the "veiled head" shilling was designed by Sir Thomas Brock. The reverse, which shows three shields in the form of a trefoil within the Garter, was designed by Sir Edward Paynter. Dies were engraved by G. W. de Saulles.

One variety of 1893 has smaller than normal lettering on the obverse.

Date	Quantity Minted Proof	Regular	Good	Fine	V. F.	Ex. F.	Unc.	Proof
1893...(1,312)		7,039,074	$ .75	$1.25	$3.00	$10.00	$16.00	$70.00
1894		5,953,152	1.00	2.00	5.00	15.00	22.00	
1895		8,880,651	.85	1.50	4.00	14.00	20.00	
1896		9,264,551	.75	1.25	3.00	10.00	16.00	
1897		6,270,364	.75	1.25	3.00	10.00	16.00	
1898		9,768,703	.75	1.25	3.00	10.00	16.00	
1899		10,965,382	.75	1.25	3.50	12.00	18.00	
1900		10,937,590	.75	1.25	3.00	8.00	14.00	
1901		3,426,294	.75	1.25	3.00	8.00	14.00	

Edward VII 1901-1910

Only one type of shilling was issued during this short reign. It was designed by G. W. de Saulles. Matte proofs were issued with the specimen sets in 1902.

1902..(15,123)	7,809,481	.75	1.25	3.00	14.00	20.00	50.00
1903	2,061,823	1.25	3.50	15.00	40.00	80.00	
1904	2,040,161	1.00	2.50	10.00	30.00	60.00	
1905	488,390	10.00	20.00	60.00	150.00	400.00	
1906	10,791,025	.75	1.50	4.00	16.00	25.00	
1907	14,083,418	1.00	2.00	6.50	20.00	40.00	
1908	3,806,969	1.00	2.25	10.00	37.00	80.00	
1909	5,664,982	1.00	2.25	8.00	30.00	75.00	
1910	26,547,236	.75	1.25	3.50	15.00	22.00	

Silver Shillings

George V 1910-1936

The obverse portrait was prepared from a plaster cast made by Sir Bertram Mackennal. His initials BM appear on the truncation of the bust. The first reverse design is that by de Saulles used for the previous reign.

In 1926 the effigy of the King was slightly altered; the initials were changed, the head made smaller and a new beaded border added. A new reverse, designed by Kruger Gray, was introduced in 1927.

Date	Quantity Minted Proof	Regular	Fine	V. F.	Ex. F.	Unc.	Proof
1911	(6,007)	20,065,901	$ .80	$2.00	$8.00	$16.00	$75.00
1912		15,594,009	1.00	3.00	12.00	20.00	
1913		9,011,509	4.00	7.00	25.00	60.00	
1914		23,415,843	.75	1.50	6.00	15.00	
1915		39,279,024	.60	1.25	5.00	10.00	
1916		35,862,015	.60	1.25	5.00	10.00	
1917		22,202,608	.80	2.00	8.00	16.00	
1918		34,915,934	.60	1.25	5.00	12.00	
1919		10,823,824	.75	1.75	7.00	16.00	

Debased Silver

Diameter: 23.60mm; weight: 5.66 grams; composition: *1920*, .500 silver, .400 copper, .100 nickel; *1921*, .500 silver, .450 copper, .050 manganese; *1922-1927*, .500 silver, .500 copper; edge: reeded.

1920	22,825,142	1.00	3.00	14.00	25.00
1921	22,648,763	1.00	3.00	14.00	25.00
1922	27,215,738	1.00	3.00	15.00	27.50
1923	14,575,243	1.00	3.00	15.00	27.50
1924	9,250,095	3.00	5.00	20.00	40.00
1925	5,418,764	4.00	7.00	30.00	70.00
1926 variety I	} 22,516,453	1.00	3.50	16.00	30.00
1926 variety II		1.00	3.00	12.00	20.00
1927	9,262,344	1.00	3.00	14.00	25.00

Second Type 1927-1936

Diameter: 23.60mm; weight: 5.66 grams; composition: .500 silver, .400 copper, .050 nickel, .050 zinc; edge: reeded.

1927	(15,000)	incl. above	.80	2.00	8.00	16.00	45.00

Date	Type	Quantity Minted Proof	Regular	Fine	V. F.	Ex. F.	Unc.	Proof
1928			18,136,778	$ .50	$1.00	$4.00	$10.00	
1929			19,343,006	.50	1.00	4.00	10.00	
1930			3,137,092	2.00	5.00	20.00	40.00	
1931			6,993,926	.60	1.25	5.00	12.00	
1932			12,168,101	.60	1.25	5.00	12.00	
1933			11,511,624	.60	1.25	5.00	12.00	
1934			6,138,463	1.00	3.00	15.00	30.00	
1935			9,183,462	.50	1.00	4.00	10.00	

Edward VIII 1936

All of the coins dated 1936 were technically issued for Edward VIII. These coins, however, have the exact same design and inscription as the previous issue.

Date	Regular	Fine	V.F.	Ex.F.	Unc.
1936	11,910,613	.50	1.00	4.00	10.00

George VI 1936-1952

The portrait on all coins of George VI was designed by T. H. Paget, whose initials H.P. appear on the obverse. Two different reverses are used each year. Both the English and the Scottish type reverses were designed by Kruger Gray.

The English reverse shows the British lion. The Scottish shilling was issued as a compliment to the Queen's Scottish ancestry. It has the Scottish lion seated above the crown, holding a sword in one paw and a sceptre in the other. At the sides are shields bearing St. Andrew's cross and the Scottish thistle.

In 1947 a new coinage was issued made of copper-nickel, an alloy of 75 per cent copper and 25 per cent nickel. The old 50-50 silver alloy coinage was withdrawn from circulation and used to repay silver borrowed under Lend-Lease during the war.

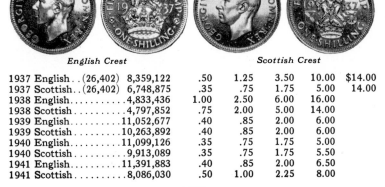

English Crest   *Scottish Crest*

Date	Quantity Minted	Fine	V.F.	Ex.F.	Unc.	Proof
1937 English..(26,402)	8,359,122	.50	1.25	3.50	10.00	$14.00
1937 Scottish..(26,402)	6,748,875	.35	.75	1.75	5.00	14.00
1938 English	4,833,436	1.00	2.50	6.00	16.00	
1938 Scottish	4,797,852	.75	2.00	5.00	14.00	
1939 English	11,052,677	.40	.85	2.00	6.00	
1939 Scottish	10,263,892	.40	.85	2.00	6.00	
1940 English	11,099,126	.35	.75	1.75	5.00	
1940 Scottish	9,913,089	.35	.75	1.75	5.50	
1941 English	11,391,883	.40	.85	2.00	6.50	
1941 Scottish	8,086,030	.50	1.00	2.25	8.00	

Copper-Nickel Shillings

Date	Type	Quantity Minted Proof	Regular	V. F.	Ex. F.	Unc.	Proof
1942 English			17,453,643	$ .50	$1.50	$5.00	
1942 Scottish			13,676,759	.75	2.00	7.00	
1943 English			11,404,213	.35	1.00	4.00	
1943 Scottish			9,824,214	.35	1.00	4.50	
1944 English			11,586,751	.35	1.00	4.00	
1944 Scottish			10,900,167	.35	1.00	4.00	
1945 English			15,143,404	.35	.75	3.50	
1945 Scottish			15,106,270	.35	.75	3.50	
1946 English			18,663,797	.35	.75	3.50	
1946 Scottish			16,381,501	.35	.75	3.50	

Copper-Nickel Coinage

Diameter: 23.60mm; weight: 5.66 grams; composition: .750 copper, .250 nickel; edge: reeded.

1947 English			12,120,611	.75	2.00	7.00	
1947 Scottish			12,283,223	.75	2.00	7.00	
1948 English			45,576,923	.75	2.00	7.00	
1948 Scottish			45,351,937	.75	2.00	7.00	

English: IND.IMP. *Omitted*   *Scottish:* IND:IMP *Omitted*

IND: IMP was omitted from the legend beginning in 1949 to signify the independence of India.

Two trial pieces dated 1952, with the English reverse, are known to exist. All other shillings coined in 1952 were dated 1953 and bear the portrait of Elizabeth II.

1949 English			19,328,405	.50	1.50	5.00	
1949 Scottish			21,243,074	.50	1.50	5.00	
1950 English		(17,513)	19,243,872	.50	1.75	6.50	$12.00
1950 Scottish		(17,513)	14,299,601	.50	1.75	6.50	12.00
1951 English		(20,000)	9,956,930	.50	1.75	6.50	12.00
1951 Scottish		(20,000)	10,961,174	.50	1.75	6.50	12.00

Elizabeth II 1952-

The portrait of Queen Elizabeth was modeled by Mrs. Mary Gillick. The practice of issuing two designs concurrently for the shilling was continued in this reign. The emblems used are the English and the Scottish quarterings of the royal arms, each designed and modeled by W. Gardner. As with all other denominations, the title was changed in 1954 to eliminate BRITT: OMN:.

[70]

English Shield   Scottish Shield

Date	Type	Quantity Minted Proof	Regular	Ex. F.	Unc.	Proof
1953 English	(40,000)	41,942,894	$ .60	$2.50	$10.00
1953 Scottish	(40,000)	20,663,528	.60	2.50	10.00

BRITT:OMN: Omitted

English Shield   Scottish Shield

1954 English	30,262,032	.50	2.25	
1954 Scottish	26,771,735	.50	2.25	
1955 English	45,259,908	.50	2.25	
1955 Scottish	27,950,906	.50	2.25	
1956 English	44,907,008	.75	4.00	
1956 Scottish	42,853,639	.75	4.00	
1957 English	42,774,217	.40	2.00	
1957 Scottish	17,959,988	2.50	16.00	
1958 English	14,392,305	2.25	17.00	
1958 Scottish	40,822,557	.30	1.75	
1959 English	19,442,778	.30	2.00	
1959 Scottish	1,012,988	3.50	18.00	
1960 English	27,027,914	.40	2.00	
1960 Scottish	14,376,932	.40	2.00	
1961 English	39,816,907	.30	1.75	
1961 Scottish	2,762,558	1.25	7.00	
1962 English	36,704,379	.25	.75	
1962 Scottish	18,967,310	.30	1.50	
1963 English	44,714,000	.25	.60	
1963 Scottish	32,300,000	.25	.60	
1964 English	8,590,900	.25	.60	
1964 Scottish	5,239,100	.25	1.00	
1965 English	9,216,000	.25	.60	
1965 Scottish	2,774,000	.25	1.00	
1966 English	15,002,000	.25	.60	
1966 Scottish	15,604,000	.25	.60	
1970 English issued only in sets				2.50
1970 Scottish issued only in sets				2.50

SILVER FLORINS
Victoria 1837-1901

A florin is equal to two shillings. The term was first used to designate a coin from the city of Florence, Italy. The florin was first proposed in 1848 by William Wyon as an answer to popular demand for a decimal coinage. A large number of pattern coins of the value of one-tenth of a pound were struck. The design adopted for issue the following year did not have the traditional DEI GRATIA in the title and became known as the "Godless and Graceless" florin. The reverse was designed by W. Dyce.

Diameter: 27.70mm; weight: 11.31 grams; composition: .925 silver, .075 copper; edge: reeded.

"Godless" Florin

Date	Quantity	Fine	V. F.	Ex. F.	Unc.	Proof
1848 type of 1849	Pattern					$400.00
1849	413,820	$10.00	$22.00	$45.00	$75.00	

Gothic Type Florin

The two designers of the "Godless" florin altered their designs somewhat, and in 1851, issued the beautiful "Gothic" florin. One unique feature about this coin is the date, which is in Roman numerals and in Gothic script.

Many of the florins from 1864 to 1878 have a small die number below the bust. Numbers started with one each year and changed on each new die. Several minor modifications in the design can be noted throughout this coinage. Proof specimens were struck nearly every year and all of these are very rare.

After 1867 the legend reads BRITT instead of BRIT.

Diameter: 28.50mm; weight: 11.31 grams; composition: .925 silver, .075 copper; edge: reeded.

Only the Roman numeral date is shown on these coins.	Quantity Minted	Good	Fine	V. F.	Ex. F.	Unc.
1851 mdcccli	1,540	$75.00	$200.00	$400.00	$900.00	——
1852 mdccclii	1,014,552	3.00	9.00	20.00	50.00	$90.00
1853 mdcccliii	3,919,950	3.00	10.00	22.00	55.00	100.00
1854 mdcccliv	550,413	50.00	150.00	300.00	700.00	——
1855 mdccclv	831,017	4.00	11.00	25.00	60.00	110.00
1856 mdccclvi	2,201,760	5.00	14.00	30.00	75.00	140.00
1857 mdccclvii	1,671,120	4.00	11.00	25.00	60.00	110.00
1858 mdccclviii	2,239,380	3.00	10.00	22.00	55.00	100.00
1859 mdccclix	2,568,060	4.00	11.00	25.00	60.00	110.00
1860 mdccclx	1,475,100	5.00	15.00	35.00	85.00	170.00
1862 mdccclxii	594,000	10.00	30.00	100.00	250.00	400.00
1863 mdccclxiii	938,520	12.00	35.00	125.00	350.00	450.00
1864 mdccclxiv	1,861,200	4.00	11.00	25.00	60.00	110.00
1865 mdccclxv	1,580,044	5.00	14.00	30.00	80.00	150.00
1866 mdccclxvi	914,760	5.00	14.00	30.00	80.00	150.00
1867 mdccclxvii	423,720	8.00	20.00	75.00	200.00	350.00
1868 mdccclxviii	896,940	4.00	11.00	25.00	60.00	110.00
1869 mdccclxix	297,000	3.00	10.00	22.00	55.00	100.00
1870 mdccclxx	1,080,648	3.00	10.00	22.00	55.00	100.00
1871 mdccclxxi	3,425,605	3.00	10.00	22.00	55.00	100.00
1872 mdccclxxii	7,199,690	3.00	9.00	20.00	50.00	85.00
1873 mdccclxxiii	5,921,839	3.00	9.00	20.00	50.00	85.00
1874 mdccclxxiv	1,642,630	3.00	10.00	22.00	55.00	100.00
1874 iv of date over iii.		8.00	20.00	75.00	200.00	350.00
1875 mdccclxxv	1,117,030	4.00	11.00	25.00	60.00	110.00
1876 mdccclxxvi	580,034	4.00	11.00	25.00	65.00	120.00
1877 mdccclxxvii	682,292	4.00	11.00	25.00	65.00	120.00
1877 mdccclxxvii• no ww		9.00	25.00	80.00	225.00	375.00
1878 mdccclxxviii	1,786,680	4.00	11.00	25.00	65.00	120.00
1879 mdccclxxix no ww	1,512,247	5.00	15.00	35.00	85.00	160.00
1879 mdccclxxix w/ww		5.00	14.00	30.00	80.00	140.00
1880 mdccclxxx	2,167,170	3.00	10.00	22.00	55.00	100.00
1881 mdccclxxxi	2,570,337	3.00	9.00	20.00	50.00	90.00
1881 mdccclxxri (broken x)		5.00	14.00	30.00	80.00	150.00
1883 mdccclxxxiii	3,555,667	3.00	9.00	20.00	50.00	85.00
1884 mdccclxxxiv	1,447,379	3.00	9.00	20.00	50.00	85.00
1885 mdccclxxxv	1,758,210	3.00	9.00	20.00	50.00	85.00
1886 mdccclxxxvi	591,773	3.00	10.00	22.00	55.00	100.00
1887 mdccclxxxvii	1,776,903	7.00	18.00	40.00	100.00	200.00

Silver Florins

The Jubilee head was used on the florins from 1887 through 1892. The obverse was designed by J. Boehm and the reverse by L. C. Wyon. Proofs were issued in sets in 1887 and singly in 1892.

Diameter: 28.50mm; weight: 11.31 grams; composition: .925 silver, .075 copper; edge: reeded.

Jubilee Head

Date	Quantity Minted Proof	Quantity Minted Regular	Good	Fine	V. F.	Ex. F.	Unc.	Proof
1887	(1,084)	incl. above	$1.50	$3.00	$6.00	$10.00	$20.00	$85.00
1888		1,547,540	1.75	4.00	8.00	22.00	35.00	
1889		2,973,561	1.75	4.00	8.00	22.00	35.00	
1890		1,684,737	2.00	5.00	15.00	40.00	150.00	
1891		836,438	3.00	10.00	25.00	50.00	225.00	
1892		283,401	5.00	15.00	35.00	70.00	300.00	500.00

The obverse of the "veiled head" florin was designed by Sir Thomas Brock. The reverse is very similar to the shilling and shows three shields in the form of a trefoil within the Garter. It was designed by Sir Edward Poynter. Dies were engraved by G. W. de Saulles. The 1893 proof coins were issued in the sets.

Veiled Head

Date	Proof	Regular	Good	Fine	V. F.	Ex. F.	Unc.	Proof
1893	(1,312)	1,666,103	1.75	3.50	7.00	22.00	35.00	100.00
1894		1,952,842	2.25	5.00	12.00	30.00	50.00	
1895		2,182,968	2.25	5.00	12.00	30.00	50.00	
1896		2,944,416	2.00	4.00	9.00	25.00	40.00	
1897		1,699,921	1.75	3.50	7.00	22.00	35.00	
1898		3,061,343	2.00	4.00	9.00	25.00	40.00	
1899		3,966,953	2.00	4.00	9.00	25.00	40.00	
1900		5,528,630	1.75	3.50	7.00	22.00	35.00	
1901		2,648,870	1.75	3.50	7.00	22.00	35.00	

Edward VII 1901-1910

The portrait of King Edward was by de Saulles, as was the new and attractive reverse design. It is interesting to note that the standing figure of Britannia was originally drawn from life. The daughter of the then Master of the Mint posed for de Saulles. The proof coins of 1902 have a dull, matte finish.

Date	Quantity Minted Proof	Regular	V. Good	Fine	V. F.	Ex. F.	Unc.	Proof
1902	(15,123)	2,189,575	$2.50	$5.00	$12.00	$30.00	$50.00	$70.00
1903		1,995,298	4.00	10.00	22.00	60.00	100.00	
1904		2,769,932	5.00	12.00	30.00	75.00	125.00	
1905		1,187,596	8.00	20.00	50.00	150.00	300.00	
1906		6,910,128	3.00	6.00	15.00	40.00	75.00	
1907		5,947,895	3.50	7.00	17.50	50.00	90.00	
1908		3,280,010	4.50	11.00	25.00	75.00	125.00	
1909		3,482,829	3.50	8.00	20.00	60.00	100.00	
1910		5,650,713	2.50	5.00	13.00	35.00	70.00	

George V 1910-1936

Sir Bertram Mackennal designed the portrait used throughout this coinage. The reverse of this florin was an internal mint design based on the Queen Victoria florin of the Jubilee issue. As with the other denominations, the effigy was modified in 1927 and a new reverse was introduced. The designer was Kruger Gray. Proofs were issued in sets in 1911 and 1927. The silver content of the florin was debased, in 1920 and thereafter, to one half silver and one half alloy.

Silver Florins

Date	Quantity Minted Proof	Quantity Minted Regular	V.Good	Fine	V. F.	Ex. F.	Unc.	Proof
1911	(6,007)	5,951,284	$2.00	$3.25	$7.00	$17.50	$40.00	$75.00
1912		8,571,731	2.00	4.00	8.50	20.00	50.00	
1913		4,545,278	2.50	5.00	12.00	35.00	75.00	
1914		21,252,701	1.50	2.00	3.00	12.00	20.00	
1915		12,367,939	1.50	2.00	3.00	12.00	20.00	
1916		21,064,337	1.50	2.00	3.00	12.00	20.00	
1917		11,181,617	1.75	3.00	5.00	16.00	30.00	
1918		29,211,792	1.50	2.00	3.00	12.00	20.00	
1919		9,469,292	1.75	3.00	5.00	16.00	30.00	

Debased Silver

Diameter: 28.50mm; weight: 11.31 grams; composition: *1920*, .500 silver, .400 copper, .100 nickel; *1921*, .500 silver, .450 copper, .050 manganese; *1922-1926*, .500 silver, .500 copper; edge: reeded.

1920	15,387,833	1.25	2.50	6.00	20.00	50.00
1921	34,863,895	1.25	2.00	5.00	16.00	35.00
1922	23,861,044	1.25	2.00	5.00	16.00	35.00
1923	21,546,533	1.00	1.50	3.00	12.00	22.50
1924	4,582,372	1.25	2.00	5.00	17.50	45.00
1925	1,404,136	3.50	9.00	30.00	90.00	150.00
1926	5,125,410	1.25	2.00	5.00	17.50	45.00
1927	116,497	None known to exist.				

Diameter: 28.50mm; weight: 11.31 grams; composition: .500 silver, .400 copper, .050 nickel, .050 zinc; edge: reeded.

New Design 1927-1936

1927	(15,000) Proof only						65.00
1928	11,087,186	.50	1.00	1.50	6.00	15.00	
1929	16,397,279	.50	1.00	1.50	6.00	15.00	
1930	5,753,568	.75	1.25	2.00	8.00	25.00	
1931	6,556,331	.75	1.25	2.00	7.00	20.00	
1932	717,041	3.00	6.00	15.00	75.00	140.00	
1933	8,685,303	.50	1.00	1.50	6.00	17.50	
1935	7,540,546	.50	1.00	1.50	6.00	15.00	

Edward VIII 1936

All florins dated 1936 belong to the reign of Edward VIII despite the fact that they have the title and portrait of George V. No special coins for King Edward were issued before the abdication.

1936	9,897,448	.50	1.00	1.50	5.00	12.00

George VI 1936-1952

T, H. Paget designed the obverse of the George VI florin. The reverse, showing a large English rose crowned, with thistle and shamrock at the sides, and G R (Georgius Rex) below, was designed by Kruger Gray. All silver coinage was discontinued in 1946 and existing coins were withdrawn from circulation, the silver being used for payment of war loans. Coins minted in 1947 and thereafter were made of copper-nickel. The design remained the same, but a new, closer type of reeding was used around the edge of the coins.

Date	Proof	Regular	Fine	V. F.	Ex. F.	Unc.	Proof
1937	(26,402)	13,006,781	$ .50	$1.25	$3.00	$9.00	$20.00
1938		7,909,388	1.00	3.50	8.00	25.00	
1939		20,850,607	.50	1.25	3.00	9.00	
1940		18,700,338	.50	1.25	2.50	7.00	
1941		24,451,079	.50	1.25	2.50	8.00	
1942		39,895,243	.50	1.00	2.00	5.00	
1943		26,711,987	.50	1.00	2.00	5.00	
1944		27,560,005	.50	1.00	2.00	5.00	
1945		25,858,049	.50	1.00	2.00	5.00	
1946		22,300,254	.50	1.00	2.00	5.00	

(column header above the two quantity columns reads "Quantity Minted")

Copper-Nickel Coinage

Diameter: 28.50mm; weight: 11.31 grams; composition: .750 copper, .250 nickel: edge: reeded.

Date	Proof	Regular	Fine	V. F.	Ex. F.	Unc.	Proof
1947		22,910,085	.50	1.00	2.50	7.00	
1948		67,553,636	.50	1.00	2.00	6.00	

In 1948 the King relinquished his title of INDIAE IMPERATOR (Emperor of India) and all of his coins were redesigned to eliminate the words IND: IMP:, starting with the year 1949.

Date	Proof	Regular	Fine	V. F.	Ex. F.	Unc.	Proof
1949		28,614,939	.70	1.25	2.50	7.00	
1950	(17,513)	24,357,490	.70	1.25	3.00	8.00	14.00
1951	(20,000)	27,411,747	.70	1.25	3.00	8.00	14.00

Copper-Nickel Florins

Elizabeth II 1952-

The "Royal Effigy" of Queen Elizabeth is the work of Mrs. Mary Gillick. The first dies of 1953 produced coins of rather poor relief and had to be improved in several stages of retouching and sharpening. The reverse was designed by Edgar Fuller and modeled by Cecil Thomas. It shows a double rose in the center within a circlet of radiating thistles, shamrocks and leeks; EF and CT in the field. This is the first time that the leek has appeared on a coin. It is used to represent Wales. The title BRITT:OMN: was omitted from the legend in 1954 and thereafter. Coins dated 1970 were issued only in sets.

Type of 1953

Date	Quantity Minted Proof	Regular	V. F.	Ex. F.	Unc.	Proof
1953	(40,000)	11,958,710	$ .50	$1.50	$4.50	$12.00

BRITT: OMN: *Omitted 1954-1970*

1954	13,085,422	1.50	6.00	25.00
1955	25,887,253	.50	1.50	4.50
1956	47,824,500	.50	1.50	4.50
1957	33,071,282	1.00	4.00	20.00
1958	9,564,580	.75	3.00	12.00
1959	14,080,319	1.25	5.00	22.00
1960	13,831,782		1.00	3.50
1961	37,735,315		1.00	3.50
1962	35,147,903		.60	2.25
1963	25,562,000		.60	2.25
1964	16,539,000		.50	2.00
1965	48,163,000		.40	1.25
1966	83,999,000		.40	1.25
1967	39,718,000		.40	1.25
1970 issued only in sets				3.00

SILVER HALF CROWNS
George III 1760-1820

During the years 1810-1812 the present Royal Mint was built and powerful machinery was erected by Boulton and Watt. In 1816 a complete new issue of coinage was started. Half crowns, shillings and sixpences were struck during this year. The silver issue is of reduced size and weight, being now sixty-six shillings instead of sixty-two to the troy pound. This size and weight continued up to the present and all silver from 1816 was legally current until 1971.

Thomas Wyon, Jr., who was appointed assistant engraver in 1811, became Chief Engraver in 1815; he died two years later. He designed the first or "bull head" half crown reverse and engraved the obverse from a model by Benedetto Pistrucci. After Wyon's death, Pistrucci engraved the dies himself.

Diameter: 32.31mm; weight: 14.14 grams; composition: .925 silver, .075 copper; edge: reeded.

"Bull Head" Half Crown

Date	Quantity Minted	Good	Fine	V. Fine	Ex. Fine	Unc.	Proof
1816 . . . . }	8,092,656	$5.00	$12.00	$20.00	$50.00	$100.00	$250.00
1817 . . . . }		5.00	12.00	20.00	50.00	100.00	250.00

Second Type; Smaller Head

Date	Quantity Minted	Good	Fine	V. Fine	Ex. Fine	Unc.	Proof
1817	incl. above	5.00	12.00	20.00	50.00	100.00	250.00
1818	2,905,056	5.00	12.00	20.00	50.00	100.00	250.00
1819 9 over 8 . . }	4,790,016					———	
1819 . . . . }		5.00	12.00	20.00	50.00	100.00	250.00
1820	2,396,592	6.00	15.00	25.00	60.00	125.00	250.00

Silver Half Crowns

George IV 1820-1830

The obverse showing the laureate head of King George IV was designed and engraved by Benedetto Pistrucci. The reverse of all three designs for the half crown was the work of his assistant Jean Baptiste Merlen. The engraver's initials are found hidden in the beading around the rim.

First Reverse 1820-1823

Date	Quantity Minted	Good	Fine	V. F.	Ex. F.	Unc.	Proof
1820..........incl. above		$6.00	$15.00	$30.00	$70.00	$150.00	$300.00
1821..........1,435,104		6.00	15.00	30.00	70.00	150.00	300.00
1823..........2,003,760		50.00	125.00	250.00	500.00	750.00	

Second Reverse 1823-1824

1823..........incl. above	6.00	15.00	30.00	70.00	150.00	250.00
1824............465,696	7.00	17.50	40.00	90.00	175.00	300.00

When the King's portrait was changed in 1824, Pistrucci was commissioned to engrave the obverse dies from a bust by Sir Francis Chantrey. When he refused to copy the work of another artist, the task was given to W. Wyon who produced his fine "bare head." The new reverse was engraved by Merlen.

Date	Quantity Minted	Good	Fine	V. F.	Ex. F.	Unc.	Proof
1824........incl. above		Extremely rare.					
1825..........2,258,784		$5.00	$12.00	$20.00	$50.00	$100.00	$400.00
1826..........2,189,088		5.00	12.00	20.00	50.00	100.00	350.00
1828.............49,890		6.00	16.00	32.00	80.00	175.00	
1829...........508,464		6.00	15.00	30.00	70.00	170.00	

William IV 1830-1837

The half crown dies for this reign were prepared by William Wyon, who engraved the obverse portrait from a bust by Chantrey, and J. B. Merlen, who designed and engraved the reverse. Ordinary half crowns of 1831 were struck and a few are known to exist. They were, however, never put into general circulation.

		Good	Fine	V. F.	Ex. F.	Unc.	Proof
1831 (issued in the sets)							600.00
1834 with ww...		6.00	15.00	35.00	85.00	175.00	
1834 with *ww* in script...	}993,168	5.00	12.00	25.00	60.00	100.00	
1835............281,952		10.00	20.00	50.00	100.00	200.00	
1836 6 over 5.	}1,588,752	20.00	50.00	100.00	200.00		
1836.........		5.00	12.00	25.00	60.00	100.00	
1837............150,526		6.00	15.00	30.00	75.00	150.00	

Victoria 1837-1901

William Wyon designed and engraved the "young head" of Victoria, and J. B. Merlen designed the reverse die. The design was modified occasionally during the period from 1839 to 1850 but the changes are minor. Proofs or pattern coins only were struck in 1851, 1853, 1862 and 1864. No regular half crowns were struck for circulation between 1851 and 1873. Specimens dated 1861, 1866, 1868 and 1871 exist, but their origin is not known.

Young Head – First Issue 1839-1864

Silver Half Crowns

Date	Quantity Minted	Good	Fine	V. F.	Ex. F.	Unc.	Proof
1839				$200.00	$500.00	$900.00	$500.00
1840	386,496	$10.00	$25.00	75.00	150.00	200.00	
1841	42,768	12.00	35.00	100.00	350.00	450.00	
1842	486,288	8.00	15.00	30.00	125.00	175.00	
1843	454,608	10.00	30.00	80.00	250.00	325.00	
1844	1,999,008	6.00	12.00	25.00	100.00	150.00	
1845	2,231,856	6.00	12.00	25.00	100.00	150.00	
1846	1,539,668	8.00	15.00	30.00	125.00	175.00	
1848	367,488	12.00	35.00	100.00	375.00	475.00	
1848 8 over 6		12.00	35.00	100.00	350.00	450.00	
1849 lg. date	261,360	9.00	17.50	50.00	150.00	200.00	
1849 sm. date		9.00	17.50	50.00	150.00	250.00	
1850	484,613	9.00	17.50	50.00	150.00	225.00	700.00
1851 Proof only							900.00
1853 Proof only							700.00
1862 Proof only							900.00
1864 Proof only							900.00

The second issue of "young head" half crowns minted from 1874 through 1887 has the Queen's head moulded in much lower relief than the first issue. These coins appear almost crude in comparison with the earlier pieces. The lower relief was adopted because it was found that the dies lasted much longer than previously.

Young Head – Second Issue 1874-1887

Date	Quantity Minted	Good	Fine	V. F.	Ex. F.	Unc.	Proof
1874	2,188,599	3.00	6.00	17.50	60.00	120.00	300.00
1875	1,113,483	3.00	6.00	17.50	60.00	120.00	300.00
1876 6 over 5	633,221	15.00	35.00	80.00	250.00	400.00	
1876		4.00	7.00	20.00	75.00	150.00	
1877	447,059	4.00	7.00	20.00	75.00	150.00	
1878	1,466,323	3.00	6.00	17.50	60.00	125.00	600.00
1879	901,356	5.00	10.00	30.00	100.00	175.00	600.00
1880	1,346,350	3.00	6.00	17.50	50.00	120.00	600.00
1881	2,301,495	2.50	5.00	15.00	50.00	100.00	500.00
1882	808,227	3.00	6.00	17.50	60.00	120.00	
1883	2,982,779	2.50	5.00	15.00	50.00	100.00	
1884	1,569,175	3.00	6.00	17.50	60.00	120.00	
1885	1,628,438	2.50	5.00	15.00	50.00	100.00	500.00
1886	891,767	2.50	5.00	15.00	50.00	100.00	600.00
1887	1,438,046	3.00	6.00	17.50	60.00	125.00	600.00

In 1887, the Queen's Golden Jubilee, the entire coinage was redesigned. The obverses were engraved by L. C. Wyon from designs by Sir J. Boehm; Wyon designed the reverse himself.

Diameter: 32.31 mm; weight: 14.14 grams; composition: .925 silver, .075 cooper; edge: reeded.

Date	Quantity Minted Proof	Regular	Good	Fine	V. F.	Ex. F.	Unc.	Proof
1887..(1,084)	incl. above		$2.00	$4.00	$7.00	$13.00	$20.00	$150.00
1888.........	1,428,787		3.00	5.00	12.00	25.00	40.00	
1889.........	4,811,954		2.00	4.00	8.00	18.00	30.00	
1890.........	3,228,111		3.00	6.00	13.00	27.50	45.00	
1891.........	2,284,632		3.50	7.00	13.00	30.00	50.00	
1892.........	1,710,946		3.50	7.00	13.00	30.00	50.00	

George William de Saulles was appointed Chief Engraver in 1893. He engraved the "veiled head" portrait from a design by Sir Thomas Brock, who also designed the reverse of the half crown. The IND.IMP. added to the Queen's titles signifies the fact that she was also Empress of India.

Date	Proof	Regular	Good	Fine	V. F.	Ex. F.	Unc.	Proof
1893..(1,312)		1,792,600	2.50	5.00	12.00	30.00	50.00	150.00
1894.........		1,524,960	3.00	6.00	15.00	40.00	60.00	
1895.........		1,772,662	2.50	5.50	14.00	35.00	55.00	
1896.........		2,148,505	2.50	5.50	14.00	35.00	55.00	
1897.........		1,678,643	2.50	5.00	12.00	30.00	50.00	
1898.........		1,870,055	2.50	5.50	14.00	35.00	55.00	
1899.........		2,863,872	2.50	5.50	14.00	35.00	55.00	
1900.........		4,479,128	2.00	4.00	10.00	25.00	45.00	
1901.........		1,516,570	2.00	4.00	10.00	25.00	45.00	

Silver Half Crowns

Edward VII 1901-1910

The half crown of Edward VII was designed by G. W. de Saulles. It depicts a shield in the center of the order of the Garter. The proof coins of 1902 were issued in sets. These all have a dull, matte surface instead of the usual highly polished finish.

Diameter: 32.31mm; weight: 14.14 grams; composition: .925 silver, .075 copper; edge: reeded.

Date	Quantity Minted Proof	Regular	Good	Fine	V. F.	Ex. F.	Unc.	Proof
1902	(15,123)	1,316,008	$2.00	$5.00	$15.00	$35.00	$60.00	$75.00
1903		274,840	20.00	50.00	125.00	500.00	750.00	
1904		709,652	10.00	25.00	75.00	225.00	350.00	
1905*		166,008	60.00	150.00	300.00	750.00	1,500	
1906		2,886,206	3.00	8.00	18.00	65.00	100.00	
1907		3,693,930	3.00	8.00	20.00	75.00	120.00	
1908		1,758,889	4.00	10.00	30.00	100.00	200.00	
1909		3,051,592	3.50	9.00	25.00	80.00	140.00	
1910		2,557,685	2.00	5.00	16.00	40.00	75.00	

*Counterfeits exist.

George V 1910-1936

The obverse portrait of George V was designed by Sir Bertram Mackennal. His initials BM appear on the truncation of the bust. The reverse is a modification of the design used throughout the previous reign. In 1926 the King's effigy was slightly altered; the initials were moved toward the rear of the truncation, the head made slightly larger and a new beaded border added. This type is often known as the "Modified Effigy."

During 1920 the price of silver rose to a point where silver coins were worth somewhat more than their face value. To prevent hoarding and melting of coins a new alloy was introduced consisting of 50 per cent silver, 40 per cent copper and 10 per cent nickel. When it was discovered that these coins became badly discolored, the alloy was changed to 50 per cent silver and 50 per cent copper.

The new type half crown introduced in 1927 uses a thistle, rose and shamrock as stops in the legend. Two interlocked crowned G's are on either side of a shield. The designer's initials KG, for Kruger Gray, are beneath the shield. Only proof coins of the new type were struck in 1927 for inclusion in the sets.

Variety I – Crown Touches Shield, 1911-1922

Date	Quantity Minted Proof	Quantity Minted Regular	Fine	V. F.	Ex. F.	Unc.	Proof
1911	(6,007)	2,914,573	$4.00	$10.00	$25.00	$60.00	$125.00
1912		4,700,789	5.00	12.00	30.00	70.00	
1913		4,090,169	5.00	12.00	30.00	70.00	
1914		18,333,003	1.75	4.00	12.00	25.00	
1915		32,433,066	1.75	4.00	10.00	20.00	
1916		29,530,020	1.75	4.00	12.00	25.00	
1917		11,172,052	2.00	6.00	18.00	35.00	
1918		29,079,592	2.00	5.00	15.00	30.00	
1919		10,266,737	2.50	8.00	20.00	40.00	

Debased Coinage

Diameter: 32.31mm; weight: 14.14 grams; composition: *1920*, .500 silver, .400 copper, .100 nickel; *1921*, .500 silver, .450 copper, .050 manganese; *1922-1927*, .500 silver, .500 copper; edge: reeded.

1920		17,982,077	2.00	6.00	18.00	35.00	
1921		23,677,889	2.00	6.00	18.00	35.00	
1922 var. I		16,396,724	2.00	6.00	20.00	37.50	

Variety II – Groove Between Crown and Shield, 1922-1927

1922 var. II		incl. above	2.00	6.00	20.00	40.00	
1923		26,308,526	1.75	4.00	12.00	25.00	
1924		5,866,294	4.00	10.00	25.00	55.00	
1925		1,413,461	8.00	35.00	100.00	200.00	
1926		}4,473,516	4.00	10.00	25.00	60.00	
1926 modified effigy			4.00	12.00	30.00	75.00	
1927		6,852,872	2.00	6.00	18.00	35.00	

Diameter: 32.31mm; weight: 14.14 grams; composition: .500 silver, .400 copper, .050 nickel, .050 zinc; edge: reeded.

1927	(15,000)	Proofs only					70.00
1928		18,762,727	1.25	2.50	6.50	15.00	

Silver Half Crowns

Date	Quantity Minted Proof	Quantity Minted Regular	Fine	V. F.	Ex. F.	Unc.	Proof
1929		17,632,636	$1.50	$3.00	$8.00	$17.50	
1930		809,051	8.00	25.00	100.00	175.00	
1931		11,264,468	1.50	3.00	8.00	17.50	
1932		4,793,643	2.00	6.00	18.00	35.00	
1933		10,311,494	1.50	3.00	8.00	17.50	
1934		2,422,399	2.50	8.00	25.00	60.00	
1935		7,022,216	1.50	3.00	8.00	17.50	

Edward VIII 1936

No coins were issued for circulation bearing the name and portrait of Edward VIII. Coins with the name and portrait of George V were, however, issued throughout the year, and as King George died early in January of 1936, they should properly be called an issue of Edward VIII.

1936		7,039,423	1.25	2.50	6.50	15.00	

George VI 1936-1952

The obverse of the half crown of George VI was modeled by T. H. Paget and the reverse was an adaptation of the design by Kruger Gray used during the previous reign. In 1947 a new coinage was issued consisting of an alloy of 75 per cent copper and 25 per cent nickel, the old silver coins being withdrawn from circulation to repay silver debts incurred under Lend-Lease during the war.

Diameter: 32.31mm; weight: 14.14 grams; composition: .500 silver, .400 copper, .050 nickel, .050 zinc; edge: reeded.

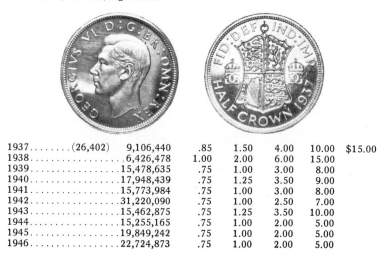

Date	Proof	Regular	Fine	V. F.	Ex. F.	Unc.	Proof
1937	(26,402)	9,106,440	.85	1.50	4.00	10.00	$15.00
1938		6,426,478	1.00	2.00	6.00	15.00	
1939		15,478,635	.75	1.00	3.00	8.00	
1940		17,948,439	.75	1.25	3.50	9.00	
1941		15,773,984	.75	1.00	3.00	8.00	
1942		31,220,090	.75	1.00	2.50	7.00	
1943		15,462,875	.75	1.25	3.50	10.00	
1944		15,255,165	.75	1.00	2.00	5.00	
1945		19,849,242	.75	1.00	2.00	5.00	
1946		22,724,873	.75	1.00	2.00	5.00	

Copper-Nickel Coinage

Diameter: 32.31mm; weight: 14.14 grams; composition: .750 copper, .250 nickel; edge: reeded.

Date	Proof	Quantity Minted Regular	V. Fine	Ex. Fine	Unc.	Proof
1947		21,911,484	$1.25	$2.50	$8.00	
1948		71,164,703	1.25	2.50	8.00	

In recognition of the independence of India, the words IND:IMP: were omitted from the legend of all coins starting in 1949. 720,370 half crowns were struck in 1952 for Elizabeth II and dated 1953. A trial piece dated 1952 with portrait of George VI is known to exist.

Date	Proof	Regular	V. Fine	Ex. Fine	Unc.	Proof
1949		28,272,512	1.00	2.50	10.00	
1950	(17,513)	28,335,500	1.00	2.50	10.00	$12.00
1951	(20,000)	9,003,520	1.00	2.50	12.00	14.00
1952		(Unique)	Not issued for circulation.			

Elizabeth II 1952-

The Queen's portrait was designed by Mrs. Mary Gillick and the reverse of this coin was designed by E. G. Fuller and modeled by Cecil Thomas. It has as its motif a square-topped shield bearing the royal arms, between a large ER; a small EF and CT are in the field. The obverse legend was altered in 1954 to eliminate BRITT:OMN: from the Royal Title.

1953   BRITT:OMN: *Omitted 1954-1970*

Date	Proof	Regular	V. Fine	Ex. Fine	Unc.	Proof
1953	(40,000)	3,883,214	.75	2.00	7.00	10.00
1954		11,614,953	1.00	5.00	20.00	
1955		23,628,726	.75	2.00	8.00	

Date	Quantity Minted Proof	Regular	V. F.	Ex. F.	Unc.	Proof
1956		33,934,909		$2.00	$9.00	
1957		34,200,563		1.00	5.00	
1958		15,745,668		7.00	20.00	
1959		9,028,844		10.00	35.00	
1960		19,929,191		1.00	5.00	
1961		25,887,897		1.00	4.00	
1962		24,013,312		.75	3.50	
1963		17,557,600		.75	3.50	
1964		5,973,600		.75	3.50	
1965		9,778,400		.75	2.50	
1966		13,375,200		.50	1.50	
1967		33,058,400		.50	1.25	
1970 issued only in sets						$3.50

SILVER DOUBLE FLORINS

In 1887 a new denomination was added to the English coinage. The double florin was never a popular coin and was issued for only four years, after which it was discontinued. Pattern two florin pieces were made in 1890, 1911 and 1914. The denomination was, however, never again approved.

The design of the double florin was an enlargement of the florin and was the work of W. Wyon and J. Boehm. Coins of 1887 have either a Roman or Arabic style figure 1 in the date. Varieties of 1888 and 1889 show a broken I in VICTORIA.

Diameter: 36mm; weight: 22.62 grams; composition: .925 silver, .075 copper; edge: reeded.

Victoria 1837-1901

Date	Quantity Minted Proof	Regular	Good	Fine	V. F.	Ex. Fine	Unc.	Proof
1887 Roman I (1,084)		⎫ 483,347	$4.00	$8.00	$15.00	$30.00	$60.00	$150.00
1887 Arabic 1		⎭	3.00	6.00	12.00	25.00	50.00	125.00
1888		⎫ 243,340	4.00	8.00	15.00	35.00	70.00	
1888 VICTORIA*		⎭	5.00	10.00	20.00	50.00	125.00	
1889		⎫ 1,185,111	4.00	8.00	15.00	30.00	60.00	
1889 VICTORIA*		⎭	6.00	12.00	25.00	60.00	150.00	
1890		782,146	4.00	8.00	15.00	30.00	65.00	

* Second I in VICTORIA broken at base.

SILVER CROWNS
George III 1760-1820

In 1797 there was an acute shortage of large size silver coins in Great Britain. No crown size pieces had been issued since 1751 during the reign of George II and all silver was being hoarded extensively. To remedy the situation the Bank of England started buying Spanish eight Real pieces or "dollars" and reissued them for circulation after countermarking them with an oval stamp bearing the head of George III. These countermarked "dollars" were valued at 4 shillings 9 pence each. They are usually coins of Charles III or Charles IV of Spain and most of them came from Spanish-American mints of Mexico City, Lima and Potosí. Smaller denominations were also counterstamped.

The countermarked "dollars" were very unpopular with the public because of their unstable value, the dislike of Spain and the flood of counterfeit pieces in circulation. In 1799, to check this counterfeiting, a new octagonal counter-mark with a larger bust of the King was used.

	Fine	V. F.	Ex. Fine
Dollar, with oval counterstamp	$75.00	$125.00	$225.00
Half dollar, with oval counterstamp	100.00	150.00	275.00
Dollar, with octagonal counterstamp	150.00	200.00	300.00

The price of silver rose to a point where the countermarked dollars had to be revalued at 5 shillings in 1800, and in 1804 it was decided to overstrike the Spanish eight Real coins with complete dies. The project was undertaken by Matthew Boulton at his foundry in Soho and the dies were prepared by

Silver Crowns

Conrad Küchler, the engraver who also made dies for the "cartwheel" copper pieces. These coins bear the inscription BANK OF ENGLAND 1804 FIVE SHILLINGS DOLLAR. They were coined in 1804, 1810 and 1811, but they were all made from dies dated 1804. Traces of the original Spanish dollars may be seen beneath the new design. Many minor varieties exist and several proof and pattern pieces were made in various metals.

Bank of England Dollar
George III 1760-1820

Date	Good	Fine	V. F.	Ex. F.	Unc.	Proof
1804 Britannia reverse...	$10.00	$25.00	$50.00	$125.00	$250.00	$400.00
1804 shield reverse......	Proof only					450.00

Silver crowns were first issued for George III in 1818. These were the first crowns to have a raised rim around the edge to protect them from wear. They have the year of the reign on the edge in Roman numerals — DECVS ET TVTA-MEN. ANNO REGNI LVIII (LIX or LX) "An ornament and a safeguard. In the year of the reign 58 (59 or 60)." Benedetto Pistrucci was the designer and engraver.

Diameter: 38.74mm; weight: 28.28 grams; composition: .925 silver, .075 copper; edge: incuse or raised lettering as noted.

Date	Edge Year	Quantity Minted	Good	Fine	V. F.	Ex. F.	Unc.	Proof
1818 LVIII......	} 155,232		$10.00	$30.00	$75.00	$175.00	$250.00	$500.00
1818 LIX.......			10.00	30.00	75.00	175.00	260.00	

Date	Edge Year	Quantity Minted	Good	Fine	V. F.	Ex. F.	Unc.	Proof
1819	LIX 9 over 8	}683,496	$10.00	$30.00	$100.00	$250.00	$350.00	
1819	LIX.......		10.00	30.00	75.00	175.00	250.00	
1819	LX........		10.00	30.00	75.00	175.00	260.00	$350.00
1820	LX							
	20 over 19.	}448,272	10.00	30.00	80.00	200.00	300.00	
1820	LX........		10.00	30.00	75.00	175.00	250.00	400.00

George IV 1820-1830

The first, or laureate head crowns of George IV, were engraved by Benedetto Pistrucci. The reverse shows his famous St. George and the dragon design. The edge inscription is in raised letters and reads, DECUS ET TUTAMEN. ANNO REGNI SECVNDO (or TERTIO) to indicate the year of the reign. Many of the proof coins have a plain edge. The 1821 issue with edge year TERTIO was made in error. A rare variety of the 1821 SECVNDO issue has the mint master's initials, WWP, inverted. Trial pieces dated 1823 are very rare.

1821 SECVNDO...	}437,976	10.00	30.00	80.00	200.00	375.00	500.00
1821 TERTIO....		Proof only					1,200
1822 SECVNDO...	}124,929	15.00	50.00	125.00	250.00	450.00	
1822 TERTIO....		12.00	40.00	100.00	225.00	400.00	500.00

Proof coins only were struck in 1826 for inclusion in the mint sets of that year. The new design was the work of William Wyon. The edge lettering is in small raised letters.

1826 SEPTIMO..........Proof only. Issued in the specimen sets.... 1,500

Silver Crowns
William IV 1830-1837

A few pattern or proof crowns were struck during the reign of William IV. None of these coins were issued for circulation. These pieces were struck in various metals and dated 1831, 1832 and 1834. All were designed by William Wyon.

Proof

1831 . . . . Proof only. Issued in the specimen sets $3,500

Victoria 1837-1901

The "young head" crown of Victoria was designed by W. Wyon, whose name appears on the truncation of the bust, above the date. The reverse was designed by his assistant, Merlen, and shows a square-topped shield, crowned, within branches and with flowers below. The Hanoverian shield was dropped from the royal arms because Victoria, being female, did not succeed to the throne of Hanover.

The year of the reign appears in incuse letters on the edge of the coin and reads: DECUS ET TUTAMEN. ANNO REGNI VIII (or XI). Some of the proof and pattern pieces have a plain edge. Proof specimens were included in the mint sets dated 1839, but none of these crowns were put into circulation. They were first issued for general circulation in 1844.

Young Head

Date	Edge Year	Quantity Minted	Good	Fine	V. F.	Ex. F.	Unc.	Proof
1839 . . . . Proof only						$700.00		$1,500
1844 VIII	94,248	$15.00	$25.00	$75.00	350.00	$500.00	1,500
1845 VIII	159,192	15.00	25.00	75.00	350.00	500.00	
1847 XI	140,976	20.00	30.00	90.00	400.00	800.00	

The Gothic style crown was issued only in 1847 and 1853. Edge inscriptions (in raised letters) refer to the year of reign. The extremely rare pieces dated

1847 with SEPTIMO on the edge are all proofs and are either errors or trial pieces struck in 1853 with the old reverse. The proof crowns dated 1853 were included in the sets but were not issued for circulation. The obverse was designed by W. Wyon and the reverse by W. Dyce. Counterfeits exist.

Gothic Style

Date	Edge Year	Quantity Minted	V. F.	Ex. F.	Unc.	Proof
1847	UNDECIMO	8,000	$300.00	$500.00	$1,000	$1,100
1847	SEPTIMO	Proof only				———
1847	plain edge	Proof only		600.00		1,200
1853	SEPTIMO	460		1,000		2,250
1853	plain edge	Proof only				———

The "Jubilee" crown was issued to celebrate the golden jubilee of the Queen's reign. Sir J. Boehm designed the portrait, and the reverse was a reinstatement of Pistrucci's famous "St. George and the dragon," which continued to be used until 1902. The jubilee head was discontinued in 1892.

Diameter: 38.74mm; weight: 28.28 grams; composition: .925 silver, .075 copper; edge: reeded.

Jubilee Head

Date	Quantity Minted Proof	Regular	Good	Fine	V. F.	Ex. Fine	Unc.	Proof
1887	(1,084)	273,581	$7.00	$10.00	$16.00	$30.00	$60.00	$350.00
1888		131,899	9.00	15.00	35.00	75.00	150.00	
1889		1,807,223	7.00	10.00	20.00	40.00	75.00	
1890		997,862	7.00	10.00	20.00	40.00	75.00	
1891		566,394	7.00	10.00	20.00	45.00	85.00	
1892		451,334	8.00	12.00	25.00	50.00	100.00	

Silver Crowns

Mint Engraver G. W. de Saulles executed the dies for the "Veiled head" of Victoria after a portrait by Sir Thomas Brock, whose initials, TB, appear below the bust. The reverse is a continuation of the St. George design by Pistrucci. The edge lettering is once again used throughout this issue. Two edge dates (year of reign) are used for each calendar date. As an example, the 1893 coins used DECUS ET TUTAMEN. ANNO REGNI LVI for the first part of the year and LVII for the last half of the year.

Diameter: 38.74mm; weight: 28.28 grams; composition: .925 silver, .075 copper; edge: raised lettering.

Veiled Head

Date	Edge Year	Quantity Minted Proof	Quantity Minted Regular	Good	Fine	V. F.	Ex. Fine	Unc.	Proof
1893 LVI	(1,312)	497,845	$7.00	$12.00	$25.00	$50.00	$150.00	$475.00
1893 LVII			8.00	15.00	30.00	65.00	175.00	
1894 LVII		144,906	8.00	15.00	30.00	65.00	175.00	
1894 LVIII			9.00	17.50	35.00	75.00	200.00	
1895 LVIII		252,862	9.00	17.50	35.00	75.00	200.00	
1895 LIX			8.00	15.00	30.00	65.00	175.00	
1896 LIX		317,599	12.00	25.00	50.00	100.00	250.00	
1896 LX			8.00	15.00	30.00	65.00	175.00	
1897 LX		262,118	8.00	15.00	30.00	65.00	175.00	
1897 LXI			7.00	12.00	25.00	50.00	150.00	
1898 LXI		161,450	15.00	30.00	65.00	125.00	275.00	
1898 LXII			8.00	15.00	30.00	65.00	175.00	
1899 LXII		166,300	8.00	15.00	30.00	65.00	175.00	
1899 LXIII			8.00	15.00	30.00	65.00	175.00	
1900 LXIII		353,356	8.00	15.00	30.00	65.00	175.00	
1900 LXIV			7.00	12.00	25.00	50.00	150.00	

Edward VII 1901-1910

Crowns of this reign were struck in only one year. The portrait was engraved by de Saulles and the reverse continues the use of Pistrucci's St. George design. The edge has the inscription DECUS ET TUTAMEN. ANNO REGNI II in raised letters. Matte proof coins were included in the sets of 1902.

Date	Quantity Minted Proof	Regular	Fine	V. F.	Ex. F.	Unc.	Proof
1902........	(15,123)	256,020	$30.00	$50.00	$100.00	$150.00	$175.00

George V 1910-1936

All of the crowns of George V are made of debased silver and contain 50 per cent alloy and 50 per cent silver. A complete departure was made from the traditional design of former years. The portrait is the work of Sir Bertram Mackennal and the reverse dies were designed by Kruger Gray. They show a large crown within a wreath of shamrock, thistles and roses.

Edge lettering was discontinued and a normal reeded edge used on this issue. The 1927 crowns were included in the proof sets only and not issued for circulation. Because of the small quantities issued each year, none of these coins are now found in actual circulation.

Diameter: 38.74mm; weight: 28.28 grams; composition: .500 silver, .400 copper, .050 nickel, .050 zinc; edge: reeded or as noted.

Date	Quantity Minted	Fine	V. F.	Ex. F.	Unc.	Proof
1927........(15,030)	Proof only			125.00		175.00
1928....................	9,034	50.00	75.00	125.00	200.00	
1929....................	4,994	60.00	80.00	150.00	225.00	
1930....................	4,847	60.00	80.00	150.00	225.00	
1931....................	4,056	65.00	90.00	175.00	250.00	
1932....................	2,395	90.00	125.00	250.00	350.00	
1933....................	7,132	60.00	80.00	150.00	225.00	
1934....................	932	300.00	450.00	850.00	1,300	

Silver Crowns

The first true British Commemorative coin was issued in 1935 to celebrate the King's silver jubilee. The very modernistic St. George design was the creation of Percy Metcalfe. The edge of the 1935 crown is inscribed in incuse letters, DECUS ET TUTAMEN. ANNO REGNI XXV. The proofs, however, have the inscription in raised letters and are made of .925 fine silver. An additional 25 pieces were struck in 22 carat gold.

Date	Quantity Minted Proof	Regular	Fine	V. F.	Ex. F.	Unc.	Proof
1935.........	(2,500)	714,769	$4.50	$7.00	$12.50	$20.00	
1935 special specimen issue. Incuse edge lettering							$50.00
1935 edge inscription in relief, .925 fine silver							300.00

Edward VIII 1936

Crowns dated 1936 were issued for Edward VIII. They bear the portrait and inscription of King George V because suitable dies were not prepared until the time of Edward's abdication and coins with his portrait were never issued. The type is identical with that issued from 1927 to 1934 and has a reeded edge.

1936.....................	2,473	100.00	150.00	250.00	350.00

George VI 1936-1952

Crowns were issued for George VI in 1937 and again in 1951. The portrait was designed by T. H. Paget whose initials appear on the obverse. The first reverse was designed by Kruger Gray and the second reverse was a reintroduction of Pistrucci's St. George.

The 1937 crown is struck in .500 fine (debased) silver and the 1951 issue is made of a copper-nickel alloy consisting of 75 parts copper and 25 parts nickel.

Date	Quantity Minted Proof	Regular	Fine	V. F.	Ex. F.	Unc.	Proof
1937........(26,402)		418,699	$8.00	$12.00	$20.00	$30.00	$60.00

The 1951 crown has a dual commemorative function. First, it commemorates the Centenary of the Great Exhibition of 1851, and secondly, it celebrates the 1951 Festival of Britain. The edge inscription MDCCCLI CIVIUM INDUSTRIA FLORET CIVITAS MCMLI translates, "1851 By the Industry Of Its People The State Flourishes 1951." A total of 2,003,540 pieces was struck and all of these were proofs. 20,000 of them were issued in sets of the year; others were issued in special boxes.

Diameter: 38.74mm; weight: 28.28 grams; composition: .750 copper, .250 nickel; edge: incuse lettering.

1951......(2,003,540) Proof only............. 6.00   12.50

Copper-Nickel Crowns

Elizabeth II 1952-

A special crown piece was struck to celebrate the coronation of Queen Elizabeth. These coins were all issued either in special plastic cases or as proofs in the sets. The obverse design is quite unlike any coin issued since the reign of Charles I and depicts the Queen sitting side-saddle on horseback and wearing the uniform of Colonel-in-Chief of the Grenadier Guards. It was designed by Gilbert Ledward. The reverse, an equally striking design, was the work of E. G. Fuller and Cecil Thomas. The incuse edge inscription reads: FAITH AND TRUST I WILL BEAR UNTO YOU.

Date	Quantity Minted Proof	Regular	V. F.	Ex. F.	Unc.	Proof
1953	(40,000)	5,962,621	$2.00	$3.00	$6.50	$30.00

The reissuance of a crown in 1960 was in celebration of the British Exhibition in New York, where a coinage press was set up and put into operation striking medallions. Special proof-like specimens of the crown were struck at the Royal Mint for distribution at the Exhibition. In addition to these pieces, a large quantity of regular crowns was struck for circulation in Great Britain. Only about 18,000 of the proof coins were distributed. The rest were bagged and circulated as regular coinage.

The Queen's portrait was designed by Mrs. Mary Gillick; the reverse remained unchanged. The edge is reeded.

Diameter: 38.74mm; weight: 28.28 grams; composition: .750 copper, .250 nickel; edge: reeded.

| 1960 . . . . | (70,000) | 1,024,038 | 3.00 | 7.00 | 10.00 | 20.00 |

The 1965 crown was issued to honor the beloved Prime Minister, Sir Winston Spencer Churchill. The obverse is similar to the 1960 issue except that the date replaces the denomination. The designer's initials, M. G., are on the truncation.

The reverse, showing a rather stern portrait of Sir Winston Churchill in his "siren-suit," was designed by Oscar Nemon. The edge is reeded. These crowns were distributed by major banks throughout the world.

Diameter: 38.74mm; weight: 28.28 grams; composition: .750 copper, .250 nickel; edge: reeded.

Date	Quantity Minted	Unc.
1965	19,640,000	$1.50

BANK OF ENGLAND TOKENS

The following series of tokens was issued by the Bank of England to alleviate the shortage of silver coins which had been caused by a rise in the price of silver during the reign of George III. These tokens were made in conjunction with the Bank of England dollars described on pages 81-82. The silver content of the tokens was somewhat lower than the required standard for Regal coins, but they did receive general acceptance.

An indication of the official status of these pieces is given in the Act of Parliament of July 29, 1812. This, and another Act dated May 25, 1813, forbade the circulation of all private tokens, with the exception of the Bank of England pieces, which continued to be issued until 1816. The overstamped and countermarked Spanish American dollars and the Bank of England silver tokens were withdrawn from circulation in 1818.

All of these tokens were made by Matthew Boulton at the Soho Mint in Birmingham, and all have plain edges. Two different obverse types were used. Approximately £4.5 million worth of these tokens was issued.

Dies were prepared for a ninepence piece, but this denomination was not put into circulation. A similiar series of tokens, in denominations of six shillings, 30 pence, tenpence and fivepence, was made for use in Ireland.

Bank of England Tokens

One Shilling Sixpence (18 Pence)

	Fine	V. F.	Ex. F.	Unc.	Proof
1811 draped bust...............	$4.00	$12.00	$25.00	$50.00	$65.00
1812 draped bust...............	4.00	12.00	25.00	50.00	65.00
1812 laureate head..............	3.00	10.00	20.00	40.00	
1813 laureate head..............	5.00	15.00	30.00	60.00	
1814 laureate head..............	3.00	10.00	20.00	40.00	
1815 laureate head..............	3.00	10.00	20.00	40.00	
1816 laureate head..............	5.00	15.00	30.00	60.00	

Three Shillings

1811 draped bust...............	6.00	18.00	35.00	70.00	100.00
1812 draped bust...............	6.00	20.00	40.00	75.00	100.00

1812 laureate head..............	5.00	15.00	30.00	65.00	125.00
1813 laureate head..............	5.00	15.00	30.00	60.00	
1814 laureate head..............	5.00	15.00	30.00	60.00	
1815 laureate head..............	5.00	15.00	30.00	60.00	
1816 laureate head..............	17.50	35.00	125.00	200.00	

[100]

SILVER MAUNDY SETS
Maundy Money

Each year the Royal Mint strikes a special series of silver coins known as Maundy money. These coins consist of a penny, twopence, threepence and fourpence. Maundy coins are always struck in .925 fine silver, with the exception of these coined from 1921 through 1946, which were struck in .500 fine silver. They are usually coined with a proof-like finish and all have a plain edge, as they are not intended for general circulation despite, the fact that they are legal tender.

The custom of distributing royal alms on Maundy Thursday — as the day before Good Friday is called — has been carried on for centuries. The Kings and Queens of former years used to wash the feet of as many beggars as the monarch had years. This part of the ceremony has not been carried on since the days of James II; the distribution of alms, however, is continued each year.

The word "Maundy" is derived from the Latin "mandatum" — mandate or command. This was the first word used in the ceremony of washing the feet of the poor people, in emulation of the Savior's action on the eve of the crucifixion, when Christ washed the feet of his disciples and gave them the "Mandatum Novum" or new commandment — "Love one another."

Special Maundy coins were first struck for Charles II in 1661. The ceremony of distributing the money is usually conducted at Westminster Abbey. Purses of Maundy money are given to one man and one woman for each year of the sovereign's age. In accordance with tradition, part of the money is contained in a white leather purse, part in a red leather purse and part in a paper packet. The money in the white purse consists of a number of pence equal to the age of the reigning sovereign.

The prices indicated in this book are for a set of one coin of each denomination for the given year and pertain to coins in perfect mint condition. Sets of coins in plush boxes and complete bags of Maundy coins are valued higher. Coinage figures pertain to the largest number of complete sets made each year and do not necessarily mean that coins of each denomination were struck in that amount.

Maundy Sets
George III 1760-1820

Fourth or Last Type, 1817-1820

Date	Ex. Fine	Mint State	Date	Ex. Fine	Mint State
1817	$65.00	$115.00	1820	$60.00	$100.00
1818	60.00	100.00			

Silver Maundy Sets

George IV 1820-1830

The die for the threepence of 1822 was made with a punch intended for the twopence. The head on this coin is, therefore, smaller than that on all other threepences. Proof sets were issued in 1822 and in 1828.

Varieteis of the 1825 and 1826 twopence show T in BRIT overpunched with B.

Date	Ex. Fine	Mint State	Date	Ex. Fine	Mint State
1822	$60.00	$90.00	1827	$50.00	$75.00
1823	50.00	75.00	1828	50.00	75.00
1824	60.00	100.00	1829	50.00	75.00
1825	50.00	75.00	1830	50.00	80.00
1826	50.00	75.00			

William IV 1830-1837

Date	Ex. Fine	Mint State	Date	Ex. Fine	Mint State
1831	60.00	90.00	1835	55.00	80.00
1832	55.00	80.00	1836	55.00	80.00
1833	55.00	80.00	1837	55.00	80.00
1834	55.00	80.00			

Victoria 1837-1901

The threepence is usually the scarcest coin in the Maundy sets after 1845. This is probably due to the fact that many of them were placed in circulation. A variety of the 1861 twopence exists with the date altered from 1811. Maundy sets were included in the proof sets of 1838, 1839, 1853, 1867, 1871, 1878, 1881 and 1888.

A quantity of twopence pieces dated 1838, 1843 and 1848 was issued for use in British Guiana and the West Indies.

Date	Number of Complete Sets	Ex. Fine	Mint State	Date	Number of Complete Sets	Ex. Fine	Mint State
1838	4,158	$47.50	$65.00	1863	4,158	$47.50	$65.00
1839	4,125	47.50	65.00	1864	4,158	42.50	65.00
1840	4,125	47.50	65.00	1865	4,158	42.50	65.00
1841	2,574	60.00	75.00	1866	4,158	42.50	65.00
1842	4,125	47.50	65.00	1867	4,158	42.50	65.00
1843	4,158	47.50	65.00	1868	4,158	42.50	65.00
1844	4,158	47.50	65.00	1869	4,158	55.00	70.00
1845	4,158	47.50	65.00	1870	4,488	42.50	65.00
1846	4,158	47.50	65.00	1871	4,488	42.50	65.00
1847	4,158	55.00	70.00	1872	4,328	42.50	65.00
1848	4,158	55.00	70.00	1873	4,162	50.00	67.50
1849	4,158	50.00	70.00	1874	4,488	42.50	65.00
1850	4,158	47.50	65.00	1875	4,154	42.50	67.50
1851	4,158	47.50	65.00	1876	4,488	42.50	60.00
1852	4,158	55.00	70.00	1877	4,488	42.50	60.00
1853	4,158	47.50	65.00	1878	4,488	42.50	60.00
1854	4,158	47.50	65.00	1879	4,488	42.50	60.00
1855	4,158	50.00	70.00	1880	4,488	42.50	60.00
1856	4,158	47.50	65.00	1881	4,488	42.50	60.00
1857	4,158	47.50	65.00	1882	4,146	47.50	67.50
1858	4,158	47.50	65.00	1883	4,488	42.50	60.00
1859	4,158	47.50	70.00	1884	4,488	42.50	60.00
1860	4,158	47.50	65.00	1885	4,488	42.50	60.00
1861	4,158	47.50	65.00	1886	4,488	42.50	60.00
1862	4,158	47.50	65.00	1887	4,488	47.50	75.00

Silver Maundy Sets

Jubilee Type

Date	Number of Complete Sets	Ex. Fine	Mint State	Date	Number of Complete Sets	Ex. Fine	Mint State
1888	4,488	$55.00	$75.00	1891	4,488	$50.00	$70.00
1889	4,488	50.00	70.00	1892	4,488	50.00	70.00
1890	4,488	50.00	70.00				

Victoria Veiled Head Type

Date	Number of Complete Sets	Ex. Fine	Mint State	Date	Number of Complete Sets	Ex. Fine	Mint State
1893	8,976	37.50	55.00	1898	9,147	35.00	50.00
1894	8,976	35.00	50.00	1899	8,976	35.00	50.00
1895	8,877	35.00	50.00	1900	8,976	35.00	50.00
1896	8,476	35.00	50.00	1901	8,976	35.00	50.00
1897	9,388	35.00	50.00				

Edward VII 1901-1910

Date	Number of Complete Sets	Ex. Fine	Mint State	Date	Number of Complete Sets	Ex. Fine	Mint State
1902	8,976	$32.50	$42.50	1907	8,760	$30.00	$40.00
1903	8,976	30.00	40.00	1908	8,760	30.00	40.00
1904	8,876	30.00	40.00	1909	1,983	40.00	50.00
1905	8,976	30.00	40.00	1910	1,440	50.00	60.00
1906	8,800	30.00	40.00				

George V 1910-1936

In 1921 the metal content of the Maundy coins was changed to 50 per cent silver and 50 per cent alloy. A change was made in the design of the regular threepences starting in 1927, but the design of the Maundy threepence remained the same except for minor modifications, so for the first time the Maundy and current threepences were of different designs. The sets of 1932 were personally distributed by the King.

1911	1,768	40.00	50.00	1916	1,128	40.00	50.00
1912	1,246	40.00	50.00	1917	1,237	40.00	50.00
1913	1,228	40.00	50.00	1918	1,375	40.00	50.00
1914	982	45.00	55.00	1919	1,258	40.00	50.00
1915	1,293	40.00	50.00	1920	1,399	40.00	50.00

Silver Maundy Sets

All Maundy coins are .925 fine silver with the exception of those made from 1921 through 1946 which are .500 fine. Weights and diameters are: *4d,* 17.63mm, 1.89 grams; *3d,* 16.26mm, 1.41 grams; *2d,* 13.44mm, 0.94 grams; *1d,* 11.15mm, 0.47 grams.

Date	Number of Complete Sets	Ex. Fine	Mint State	Date	Number of Complete Sets	Ex. Fine	Mint State
1921	1,386	$42.00	$55.00	1929	1,761	$42.00	$55.00
1922	1,373	42.00	55.00	1930	1,724	42.00	55.00
1923	1,430	42.00	55.00	1931	1,759	42.00	55.00
1924	1,515	42.00	55.00	1932	1,835	42.00	55.00
1925	1,438	42.00	55.00	1933	1,872	42.00	55.00
1926	1,504	42.00	55.00	1934	1,887	42.00	55.00
1927	1,647	42.00	55.00	1935	1,928	50.00	60.00
1928	1,642	42.00	55.00	1936*	1,323	70.00	90.00

Edward VIII 1936

*The above mentioned Maundy coins dated 1936 were actually coined for Edward VIII. They were personally distributed by him at the ceremony despite the fact that they bear the portrait and title of George V.

George VI 1936-1952

When the regular coinage was changed to copper-nickel in 1947, it was decided to once again coin the Maundy pieces in good silver as in former years. King George personally distributed Maundy money for several years. The usual change in the legend took place in 1949 after India gained independence. The Maundy coins dated 1952 were personally distributed by Queen Elizabeth II.

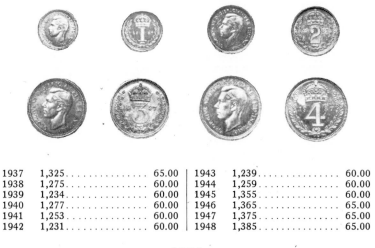

1937	1,325	65.00	1943	1,239	60.00
1938	1,275	60.00	1944	1,259	60.00
1939	1,234	60.00	1945	1,355	60.00
1940	1,277	60.00	1946	1,365	65.00
1941	1,253	60.00	1947	1,375	65.00
1942	1,231	60.00	1948	1,385	65.00

Date	Number of Complete Sets	Mint State	Date	Number of Complete Sets	Mint State
1949	1,395	$65.00	1951	1,468	$65.00
1950	1,405	65.00	1952	1,012	70.00

Elizabeth II 1952-

The legend on the Maundy coins of 1953 corresponds with the regular coins. In 1954 it was changed to eliminate BRITT: OMN: from the Queen's titles owing to the changing status of so many Commonwealth territories.

Maundy coins issued since 1971 are of the same design but are valued in new pence.

Date	Sets	Price	Date	Sets	Price
1953	1,025	200.00	1965	1,143	65.00
1954	1,020	60.00	1966	1,206	60.00
1955	1,036	65.00	1967	986	70.00
1956	1,088	60.00	1968	964	75.00
1957	1,094	65.00	1969	1,002	75.00
1958	1,100	60.00	1970	980	75.00
1959	1,106	65.00	1971	1,018	80.00
1960	1,112	60.00	1972	1,026	80.00
1961	1,118	65.00	1973	1,004	80.00
1962	1,125	60.00	1974	4,456	80.00
1963	1,131	65.00	1975		100.00
1964	1,137	60.00			

DECIMAL COINAGE

The official changeover to decimal currency took place on February 15, 1971. Prior to that date three decimal coins were circulated to introduce the new denominations.

In 1968 the five and ten new pence coins (equal to the former florin and shilling) were issued, and in 1969 the 50 new pence, equal to ten shillings, was released.

Full specimen sets of ½, 1, 2, 5 and 10 new pence were issued in 1968 as examples of the new coinage, but the bronze coins were not legalized for use until 1971.

Elizabeth II 1952-

BRONZE HALF NEW PENNY

The obverse designed by Arnold Machin shows the Queen facing right wearing a diamond tiara. Christopher Ironside designed the reverse, which depicts the Royal Crown.

Diameter: 17.14mm; weight: 1.78 grams; composition: .970 copper, .005 tin, .025 zinc; edge: plain.

Date	Quantity Minted	Ex. F.	Unc.
1971	1,394,188,250		$ .10
1973	365,680,000		.10
1974	341,888,000		.10
1975			.10

BRONZE NEW PENNY

Obverse as the half new penny by Arnold Machin. The reverse by Christopher Ironside shows the badge of King Henry VII, a portcullis with chains royally crowned.

Diameter: 20.32mm; weight: 3.56 grams; composition: .970 copper, .005 tin, .025 zinc; edge: plain.

1971	1,521,666,250		.15
1973	280,196,000		.15
1974	271,864,000		.15
1975			.15

BRONZE TWO NEW PENCE

The badge of the Prince of Wales is the central design of the reverse and is the work of Christopher Ironside. Three ostrich feathers fill a coronet of crosses pattée and fleurs de lys, with the motto ICH DIEN (I serve). Obverse is by Arnold Machin.

Diameter: 25.91mm; weight: 7.13 grams; composition: .970 copper, .005 tin, .025 zinc; edge: plain.

Date	Quantity Minted	Ex. F.	Unc.
1971	1,406,203,250		$ .20
1975			.20

Copper-Nickel Coinage

FIVE NEW PENCE

This denomination is the same size weight and composition as the shilling that it replaced.

The obverse is the same as other decimal issues designed by Arnold Machin. The reverse shows the badge of Scotland, a thistle royally crowned.

Diameter: 23.60mm; weight: 5.66 grams; composition: .750 copper, .250 nickel; edge: reeded.

1968	98,868,250	.40
1969	119,270,000	.40
1970	225,742,525	.40
1971	60,633,475	.50

Decimal Coinage

TEN NEW PENCE

Equivalent to the former florin, the reverse design of this coin is by Christopher Ironside and depicts a part of the crest of England. The royally crowned lion is passant guardant and faces left. The obverse bust of the Queen is by Arnold Machin.

Diameter: 28.50mm; weight: 11.31 grams; composition: .750 copper, .250 nickel; edge: reeded.

Date	Quantity Minted	Ex. F.	Unc.
1968	336,143,250		$ .50
1969	314,008,000		.50
1970	133,571,000		.50
1971	63,205,000		.75
1973	152,174,000		.50
1974	89,100,000		.50
1975			.50

TWENTY-FIVE NEW PENCE

This crown size coin was issued to commemorate the silver wedding anniversary of Queen Elizabeth II and Prince Philip. The design and model were by Arnold Machin.

Diameter: 38.60mm; weight: 28.28 grams; composition: .750 copper, .250 nickel. *Collector's proofs:* .925 silver, .075 copper; edge: reeded.

1972 copper-nickel	7,352,100	$1.50	2.00
1972 silver (proof in case)	100,000		50.00

Victoria Young Head 1838-1887

Date	Quantity Minted	Fine	V. F.	Ex. F.	Unc.
1838	273,341	$60.00	$120.00	$200.00	$300.00
1839	1,230	Proof only			700.00
1841	508,835	45.00	80.00	150.00	200.00
1842	2,223,352	40.00	60.00	100.00	150.00
1843	1,251,762	40.00	70.00	125.00	175.00
1844	1,127,007	40.00	70.00	125.00	175.00
1845	887,526	50.00	90.00	175.00	225.00
1846	1,063,928	40.00	70.00	125.00	175.00
1847	982,636	40.00	70.00	125.00	175.00
1848	410,595	50.00	90.00	175.00	225.00
1849	845,112	45.00	80.00	150.00	200.00
1850	179,595	80.00	200.00	400.00	500.00
1851	773,573	40.00	70.00	125.00	175.00
1852	1,377,671	40.00	60.00	100.00	150.00
1853	2,708,796	40.00	60.00	100.00	150.00
1854	1,125,144	75.00	175.00	300.00	400.00
1855	1,120,362	40.00	60.00	100.00	150.00
1856	2,391,909	40.00	60.00	100.00	150.00
1857	728,223	35.00	50.00	80.00	125.00
1858	855,578	40.00	60.00	100.00	150.00
1859	2,203,813	35.00	50.00	80.00	125.00
1860	1,131,500	35.00	50.00	80.00	125.00
1861	1,130,867	35.00	50.00	80.00	125.00
1862		55.00	100.00	200.00	300.00
1863 without die number	} 1,571,574	40.00	60.00	100.00	150.00
1863 with die number		35.00	50.00	80.00	125.00
1864	1,758,490	35.00	50.00	80.00	125.00
1865	1,834,750	35.00	50.00	80.00	125.00
1866	2,058,776	35.00	50.00	80.00	125.00
1867	992,795	40.00	60.00	100.00	150.00
1869	1,861,764	35.00	50.00	80.00	125.00
1870	1,159,544	35.00	50.00	80.00	125.00
1871	2,062,970	35.00	50.00	80.00	125.00
1871 S (Sydney mint)	unrecorded	40.00	60.00	100.00	150.00
1872	3,248,627	35.00	50.00	80.00	125.00
1872 S	356,000	40.00	60.00	100.00	150.00
1873	1,927,050	35.00	50.00	80.00	125.00
1873 M (Melbourne mint)	165,034	40.00	60.00	100.00	150.00
1874	1,884,432	35.00	50.00	80.00	125.00
1875	516,240	35.00	50.00	80.00	125.00
1875 S	unrecorded	40.00	70.00	125.00	175.00
1876	2,785,187	35.00	50.00	80.00	125.00
1877	2,197,482	35.00	50.00	80.00	125.00
1877 M	80,016	40.00	60.00	100.00	150.00
1878	2,081,941	30.00	40.00	70.00	100.00

Gold Half Sovereigns

Date	Quantity Minted	Fine	V. Fine	Ex. F.	Unc.
1879	35,201	$45.00	$80.00	$150.00	$200.00
1879 S	94,000	50.00	90.00	175.00	225.00
1880 with die number	} 1,009,049	30.00	40.00	65.00	90.00
1880 without die number		30.00	40.00	60.00	90.00
1880 S	80,000	50.00	90.00	175.00	225.00
1881 S	62,000	50.00	90.00	175.00	225.00
1881 M	42,009	55.00	100.00	185.00	240.00
1882 S	52,000	50.00	90.00	175.00	225.00
1882 M	107,522	35.00	50.00	80.00	125.00
1883	2,870,457	30.00	40.00	70.00	100.00
1883 S	220,000	30.00	40.00	70.00	100.00
1884	1,133,756	30.00	40.00	60.00	90.00
1884 M	48,009	35.00	50.00	80.00	125.00
1885	4,468,871	30.00	40.00	60.00	90.00
1885 M	11,003	55.00	100.00	200.00	300.00
1886 S	82,000	40.00	70.00	125.00	175.00
1886 M	38,008	55.00	100.00	185.00	240.00
1887 S	134,000	45.00	80.00	150.00	200.00
1887 M	64,013	40.00	70.00	125.00	175.00

The use of die numbers was discontinued after 1880. There was no coinage in 1881 or 1882 because of the rebuilding of the mint and machinery during those two years.

Branch mints (besides the mint at London) were established at Sydney (May 1855) and Melbourne (June 1872), due to the need for gold coins in commerce and the discovery of gold in Australia. During the reign of Victoria, from 1838 to 1882, some 56½ million half sovereigns were struck (54,116,322 in London, 2,170,500 in Sydney, and 393,000 in Melbourne). Many of these undoubtedly found their way into the melting pots of jewelers, for English gold coins were known to be 22 cts. fine and there was little other source for gold of known quality.

The "jubilee head" was designed by Sir J. Boehm. The reverse continues the use of a shield designed by Wyon. Half sovereigns were minted at Melbourne (M) in 1887 and 1893, and at Sydney (S) in 1887, 1891, 1892 and 1893.

Jubilee Head 1887-1893

Date	Quantity Minted Proof	Quantity Minted Regular	Fine	V. F.	Ex. F.	Unc.	Proof
1887	(797)	871,770	$30.00	$40.00	$60.00	$80.00	$350.00
1887 S			35.00	50.00	80.00	150.00	
1887 M			40.00	60.00	100.00	175.00	
1889 S		64,000	40.00	60.00	100.00	150.00	
1890		2,266,023	30.00	40.00	60.00	80.00	
1891		1,079,286	30.00	40.00	60.00	80.00	
1891 S		154,000	40.00	60.00	100.00	165.00	
1892		13,680,486	30.00	40.00	60.00	80.00	
1893		4,426,625	50.00	90.00	175.00	225.00	
1893 M		110,024	40.00	60.00	100.00	150.00	

Gold Half Sovereigns

George W. de Saulles was appointed Chief Engraver in 1893. He engraved the "veiled head" portrait from designs by Sir Thomas Brock. The reverse is a reinstatement of Pistrucci's "St. George" design. In addition to the following English coins, half sovereigns were minted at Melbourne (M), Sydney (S), and Perth (P). These branch mint pieces have the appropriate mint mark in the center of the raised ground beneath the dragon.

Veiled Head 1893-1901

Date	Quantity Minted Proof	Quantity Minted Regular	Fine	V. F.	Ex. F.	Unc.	Proof
1893	(773)	incl. above	$25.00	$35.00	$50.00	$70.00	$300.00
1893 S		250,000	30.00	40.00	70.00	100.00	
1893 M			Extremely rare.				
1894		3,794,591	25.00	35.00	50.00	70.00	
1895		2,869,183	25.00	35.00	50.00	70.00	
1896		2,946,605	25.00	35.00	50.00	70.00	
1896 M		218,946	30.00	40.00	60.00	95.00	
1897		3,568,156	25.00	35.00	50.00	70.00	
1897 S		unrecorded	30.00	40.00	60.00	80.00	
1898		2,868,527	25.00	35.00	50.00	70.00	
1899		3,361,881	25.00	35.00	50.00	70.00	
1899 M		97,221	30.00	40.00	60.00	90.00	
1900		4,307,372	25.00	35.00	50.00	70.00	
1900 M		112,920	30.00	40.00	60.00	95.00	
1900 P (Perth mint)		119,376	30.00	40.00	60.00	90.00	
1900 S		260,000	30.00	40.00	60.00	80.00	
1901		2,037,664	25.00	35.00	50.00	70.00	

Edward VII 1901-1910

King Edward's portrait was engraved by de Saulles. The reverse continues the use of the St. George type. Matte proofs were struck in 1902 for inclusion in the sets. Pistrucci's initials, BP, appear only on the coins dated 1904 to 1910.

1902	(15,123)	4,244,457	25.00	35.00	47.50	65.00	100.00
1902 S		84,000	35.00	50.00	80.00	150.00	
1903		2,522,057	25.00	35.00	47.50	65.00	
1903 S		231,000	30.00	40.00	60.00	90.00	

Gold Half Sovereigns

Date	Proof	Regular	Fine	V. F.	Ex. F.	Unc.	Proof
1904		1,717,440	$25.00	$35.00	$50.00	$70.00	
1904 P		60,030	40.00	60.00	100.00	175.00	
1905		3,023,993	25.00	35.00	47.50	65.00	
1906		4,245,437	25.00	35.00	47.50	65.00	
1906 M		82,042	30.00	40.00	70.00	100.00	
1906 S		308,000	30.00	40.00	60.00	90.00	
1907		4,233,421	25.00	35.00	47.50	65.00	
1907 M		405,034	30.00	40.00	60.00	90.00	
1908		3,996,992	25.00	35.00	47.50	65.00	
1908 M	incl. in 1907 M		30.00	40.00	60.00	90.00	
1908 P		24,668	60.00	100.00	200.00	350.00	
1908 S		538,000	30.00	40.00	60.00	80.00	
1909		4,010,715	25.00	37.50	55.00	75.00	
1909 M		186,094	30.00	40.00	60.00	80.00	
1909 P		44,022	60.00	100.00	200.00	300.00	
1910*		5,023,881	25.00	35.00	47.50	65.00	
1910 S		474,000	30.00	40.00	60.00	80.00	

George V 1910-1936

Half sovereigns of this type were minted in England for only five years. The mints of Melbourne (M), Perth (P), Sydney (S), and South Africa (SA), however, continued to strike coins of this design as late as 1926. The mint mark on these colonial coins may be found on the ground line below the dragon. Designers were Sir Bertram Mackennal (obv.) and B. Pistrucci (rev.).

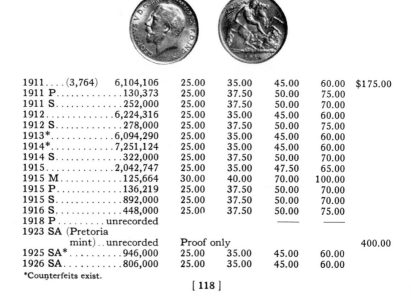

Date	Proof	Regular	Fine	V. F.	Ex. F.	Unc.	Proof
1911	(3,764)	6,104,106	25.00	35.00	45.00	60.00	$175.00
1911 P		130,373	25.00	37.50	50.00	75.00	
1911 S		252,000	25.00	37.50	50.00	70.00	
1912		6,224,316	25.00	35.00	45.00	60.00	
1912 S		278,000	25.00	37.50	50.00	75.00	
1913*		6,094,290	25.00	35.00	45.00	60.00	
1914*		7,251,124	25.00	35.00	45.00	60.00	
1914 S		322,000	25.00	37.50	50.00	70.00	
1915		2,042,747	25.00	35.00	47.50	65.00	
1915 M		125,664	30.00	40.00	70.00	100.00	
1915 P		136,219	25.00	37.50	50.00	70.00	
1915 S		892,000	25.00	37.50	50.00	70.00	
1916 S		448,000	25.00	37.50	50.00	75.00	
1918 P		unrecorded	——	——			
1923 SA (Pretoria mint)		unrecorded	Proof only				400.00
1925 SA*		946,000	25.00	35.00	45.00	60.00	
1926 SA		806,000	25.00	35.00	45.00	60.00	

*Counterfeits exist.

George VI 1936-1952

The only gold coins struck for George VI were those included in the specimen sets of 1937. All of these coins were struck as proofs and none were placed in circulation. The portrait is by T. Humphrey Paget.

Date	Quantity Minted Proof	Regular		Proof
1937............(5,501)		Proof only........................		$200.00

Elizabeth II 1952-

Gold half sovereigns were coined in the name of Elizabeth II in 1953 for inclusion in specimen sets and to maintain the series. None of these coins was ever released and the only examples extant remain in official custody. Mrs. Mary Gillick designed the Queen's portrait.

GOLD SOVEREIGNS

The gold pound, or sovereign, was first produced as a milled coin in 1817. A similar, hammered gold coin, or Broad Piece, had been last coined approximately 200 years previously under James I, and this coin was also known as a sovereign.

The new milled sovereign was smaller and thicker than the guinea that it replaced. The new coinage standard was introduced late in the reign of George III — actually during the Regency. The weight of the sovereign was established as 123.274 grains.

George III 1760-1820

The obverse shows the King's head to right, laureate, with short hair. It is the work of Benedetto Pistrucci, who also designed the St. George reverse. His initials BP are on the ground under the broken shaft of the spear.

Date	Quantity Minted	Fine	V. Fine	Ex. Fine	Unc.
1817.....................3,235,239		$110.00	$225.00	$450.00	$700.00
1818.....................2,347,230		125.00	250.00	500.00	800.00
1819 (Unique)...............3,574					
1820......................931,994		110.00	225.00	450.00	700.00

Gold Sovereigns

George IV 1820-1830

Two types of sovereigns were issued during this short reign. The first was designed by Pistrucci and depicts the King with a rather full, puffy face and wild hair crowned with a laurel wreath. At the King's request, a more flattering head was used on the coins from 1825 to 1830. This second type was copied by William Wyon from a bust by Sir Francis Chantrey. The reverse, showing a crowned shield, was by Merlen. Mint records report 386,182 sovereigns coined in 1828. Many of these were probably dated 1827, since coins dated 1828 are very rare.

Diameter: 22.05mm; weight: 7.988 grams; composition: .917 gold, .083 copper; edge: reeded.

Date	Quantity Minted	Fine	V. F.	Ex. F.	Unc.
1821	9,405,114	$125.00	$250.00	$450.00	$700.00
1822*	5,356,787	135.00	275.00	475.00	750.00
1823	616,770	350.00	600.00		
1824	3,767,904	110.00	225.00	450.00	725.00
1825*	4,200,343	350.00	700.00	1,000	1,500

Date	Quantity Minted	Fine	V. F.	Ex. F.	Unc.
1825	incl. above	125.00	250.00	450.00	700.00
1826*	5,724,046	110.00	225.00	425.00	650.00
1827	2,266,629	130.00	260.00	470.00	725.00
1828	386,182	——	——		
1829	2,444,652	130.00	260.00	475.00	750.00
1830	2,387,881	130.00	260.00	475.00	750.00

*Counterfeits exist.

William IV 1830-1837

A portrait by Sir Frances Chantrey served as a model for William Wyon, who engraved the dies for coins of William IV. The initials W.W. (for William Wyon), incused, are on the truncation of the neck. The attractive shield on the reverse was designed by Wyon's assistant, J. B. Merlen.

Gold Sovereigns

Date	Quantity Minted	Fine	V. F.	Ex. F.	Unc.
1831	598,547	$150.00	$300.00	$700.00	$1,000
1832*	3,737,065	125.00	225.00	525.00	750.00
1833	1,225,269	150.00	300.00	700.00	1,000
1835	723,441	170.00	350.00	800.00	1,200
1836	1,714,349	150.00	300.00	700.00	1,000
1837	1,172,984	140.00	275.00	650.00	900.00

*Counterfeits exist.

Victoria 1837-1901

The "young head" of Victoria was engraved by W. Wyon and copied from a model in wax taken from life. His initials WW, in relief, are on the truncation of the neck. The arms of Hanover are omitted from the shield on the reverse, designed by J. B. Merlen, because pretense to the German dominion was limited to the male line only.

Beginning with some of the 1863 issue, and continuing through 1873, die numbers were placed on the reverse under the shield. These numbers began with one at the first of each year, and were used to determine the quality of coinage from each die. It was found that approximately 100,000 coins could be stamped from a die before excess wear made discarding necessary.

Sovereigns of this type were also coined at Melbourne (M) and Sydney (S) in Australia. They can be distinguished by a mint mark below the wreath under the shield.

The St. George reverse was reintroduced in 1871 and sovereigns of both the old and the new type were issued until 1874, when the shield design was discontinued. Coinage figures include coins of both designs.

1838	2,718,694	75.00	150.00	350.00	450.00
1839	503,695	200.00	400.00	700.00	900.00
1841	124,054	1,000	1,500	2,000	——
1842	4,865,375	55.00	75.00	150.00	300.00
1843 broad shield	5,981,968	50.00	70.00	110.00	200.00
1843 narrow shield		100.00	200.00	375.00	500.00
1844	3,000,445	50.00	70.00	120.00	225.00
1844 first 4 over ♭		——			
1845	3,800,845	55.00	75.00	150.00	250.00
1846	3,802,947	50.00	70.00	110.00	200.00
1847	4,667,126	50.00	70.00	110.00	200.00
1848	2,246,701	60.00	80.00	175.00	300.00
1849	1,755,399	65.00	85.00	185.00	325.00

Gold Sovereigns

Date	Quantity Minted	Fine	V. F.	Ex. F.	Unc.
1850	1,402,039	$75.00	$100.00	$200.00	$350.00
1851	4,013,624	50.00	70.00	110.00	200.00
1852	8,053,435	50.00	70.00	100.00	185.00
1853 w.w. raised	10,597,993	50.00	70.00	100.00	185.00
1853 w.w. incuse		50.00	70.00	110.00	200.00
1854 w.w. raised	3,589,611	50.00	70.00	100.00	185.00
1854 w.w. incuse		50.00	70.00	110.00	200.00
1855 w.w. raised	8,448,482	50.00	70.00	110.00	200.00
1855 w.w. incuse		50.00	70.00	110.00	200.00
1856 normal date	4,806,160	50.00	70.00	110.00	200.00
1856 small date		50.00	70.00	100.00	185.00
1857	4,495,748	50.00	70.00	100.00	185.00
1858	803,234	75.00	125.00	250.00	400.00
1859 normal date	1,380,064	50.00	70.00	110.00	200.00
1859 small date		50.00	75.00	120.00	225.00
1859 "Ansell" variety	167,539	150.00	300.00	500.00	——

This variety can be identified by a line in the center of the hair ribbon. These coins were made by a special process to eliminate the brittleness of Australian mined gold.

Date	Quantity Minted	Fine	V. F.	Ex. F.	Unc.
1860	2,555,958	50.00	65.00	80.00	150.00
1861	7,624,736	50.00	65.00	80.00	150.00
1862	7,836,413	50.00	65.00	80.00	150.00
1863 without die number	5,921,669	50.00	65.00	80.00	150.00
1863 with die number		50.00	70.00	90.00	175.00
1864	8,656,352	50.00	65.00	75.00	150.00
1865	1,450,238	50.00	70.00	90.00	175.00
1866	4,047,288	50.00	70.00	100.00	185.00
1868	1,653,384	50.00	70.00	100.00	185.00
1869	6,441,322	50.00	70.00	90.00	175.00
1870	2,189,960	50.00	70.00	100.00	185.00
1871	8,767,250	50.00	70.00	110.00	200.00
1871 S (Sydney mint)	2,814,000	50.00	60.00	70.00	140.00
1872 without die number	13,486,708	50.00	65.00	80.00	160.00
1872 with die number		50.00	65.00	75.00	150.00
1872 M (Melbourne mint)	748,180	50.00	70.00	90.00	175.00
1872 S	1,815,000	50.00	70.00	90.00	175.00
1873	2,368,215	50.00	70.00	100.00	185.00
1873 S	1,478,000	50.00	60.00	70.00	140.00
1874	520,713	350.00	800.00	1,500	——
1874 M	1,373,298	50.00	65.00	80.00	160.00
1875 M	1,888,405			——	
1875 S	2,122,000	50.00	70.00	90.00	180.00
1877 S	1,590,000	50.00	65.00	75.00	150.00
1878 S	1,259,000	50.00	65.00	75.00	150.00
1879 S	1,366,000	50.00	65.00	75.00	150.00
1880 M	3,053,454	55.00	80.00	125.00	225.00
1880 S	1,459,000	50.00	65.00	80.00	160.00
1881 M	2,325,303	50.00	65.00	80.00	160.00
1881 S	1,360,000	50.00	65.00	75.00	150.00
1882 M	371,931	50.00	65.00	80.00	170.00
1882 S	1,298,000	50.00	65.00	75.00	150.00
1883 M	427,450	60.00	85.00	135.00	250.00
1883 S	1,108,000	50.00	65.00	80.00	160.00

Date	Quantity Minted	Fine	V. F.	Ex. F.	Unc.
1884 M	2,942,630	$50.00	$65.00	$75.00	$150.00
1884 S	1,595,000	50.00	65.00	75.00	150.00
1885 M	2,967,143	50.00	65.00	75.00	150.00
1885 S	1,486,000	50.00	65.00	75.00	150.00
1886 M	2,902,131	75.00	100.00	200.00	350.00
1886 S	1,667,000	50.00	65.00	75.00	150.00
1887 M	1,916,424	50.00	70.00	90.00	175.00
1887 S	1,000,000	50.00	65.00	75.00	150.00

Beginning in 1871, sovereigns of the Victoria young head type were issued with both the shield reverse and the St. George reverse. This practice continued until 1874, when the shield type reverse (probably made for export to India) was discontinued. The use of die numbers was abandoned on sovereigns of the new type. The designer's initials BP normally appear on the reverse of the St. George coins, but are missing on some of the dies. No gold was coined in England during 1881 and 1882 because of rebuilding of the mint.

The streamer on the helmet of St. George, which was omitted on the sovereigns of William IV, was not restored until the Jubilee issue of 1887.

From 1871 to 1887 sovereigns of this type were also minted in Australia at Melbourne (M) and Sydney (S). These coins have a mint mark on the obverse beneath the queen's head.

1871	incl. above	50.00	65.00	75.00	150.00
1871 S	incl. above	50.00	60.00	70.00	130.00
1872	incl. above	50.00	60.00	70.00	130.00
1872 M	incl. above	55.00	70.00	110.00	200.00
1872 S	incl. above	50.00	60.00	70.00	130.00
1873	incl. above	50.00	55.00	65.00	120.00
1873 M	752,199	50.00	55.00	65.00	120.00
1873 S	incl. above	50.00	60.00	70.00	140.00
1874	incl. above	60.00	75.00	150.00	300.00
1874 M	incl. above	50.00	60.00	70.00	130.00
1874 S	1,899,000	50.00	60.00	70.00	130.00
1875 M	incl. above	50.00	60.00	70.00	130.00
1875 S	incl. above	50.00	60.00	70.00	140.00
1876	3,318,866	50.00	55.00	65.00	120.00
1876 M	2,124,445	50.00	55.00	65.00	120.00
1876 S	1,613,000	50.00	60.00	70.00	130.00
1877 M	1,487,316	50.00	55.00	65.00	120.00
1878*	1,091,275	55.00	70.00	100.00	185.00
1878 M	2,171,457	50.00	55.00	65.00	120.00
1879*	20,013	175.00	350.00	750.00	1,100
1879 M	2,740,594	50.00	55.00	65.00	120.00
1879 S	incl. above	50.00	60.00	70.00	140.00
1880	3,650,080	50.00	65.00	75.00	150.00
1880 M	incl. above	50.00	55.00	65.00	120.00
1880 S	incl. above	50.00	55.00	65.00	120.00

*Counterfeits exist.

Gold Sovereigns

Date	Quantity Minted	Fine	V. F.	Ex. F.	Unc.
1881 M	incl. above	$50.00	$60.00	$70.00	$130.00
1881 S	incl. above	50.00	55.00	65.00	120.00
1882 M	2,093,850	50.00	60.00	70.00	130.00
1882 S	incl. above	50.00	55.00	65.00	120.00
1883 M	1,623,000	50.00	60.00	70.00	130.00
1883 S	incl. above	50.00	55.00	65.00	120.00
1884	1,769,635	50.00	65.00	75.00	150.00
1884 M	incl. above	50.00	55.00	65.00	120.00
1884 S	incl. above	50.00	55.00	65.00	120.00
1885	717,723	55.00	70.00	90.00	175.00
1885 M	incl. above	50.00	55.00	65.00	120.00
1885 S	incl. above	50.00	55.00	65.00	120.00
1886 M	incl. above	50.00	55.00	65.00	120.00
1886 S	incl. above	50.00	55.00	65.00	120.00
1887 M	incl. above	50.00	55.00	65.00	120.00
1887 S	incl. above	50.00	55.00	65.00	120.00

In 1887, the Queen's Golden Jubilee, it was decided that the coinage should be redesigned. The obverses were engraved by L. C. Wyon from designs by Sir J. Boehm. The reverse of the sovereign continued the use of Pistrucci's St. George and the dragon with the streamer restored to the helmet. The following coins were minted in England. Sovereigns with the same design were also minted in Australia at the Melbourne (M) and Sydney (S) mints. Proof coins of 1887 were issued in the specimen sets.

Date	Proof	Quantity Minted Regular	Fine	V. F.	Ex. F.	Unc.	Proof
1887*	(797)	1,111,280	$55.00	$65.00	$75.00	$140.00	$250.00
1887 M		940,000	50.00	55.00	65.00	110.00	
1887 S		1,002,000	50.00	55.00	65.00	110.00	
1888		2,777,424	50.00	60.00	70.00	125.00	
1888 M		2,830,612	50.00	55.00	65.00	110.00	
1888 S		2,187,000	50.00	55.00	65.00	110.00	
1889*		7,257,455	50.00	60.00	70.00	125.00	
1889 M		2,732,590	50.00	55.00	65.00	110.00	
1889 S		3,262,000	50.00	55.00	65.00	110.00	
1890		6,529,887	50.00	60.00	70.00	125.00	
1890 M		2,473,537	50.00	55.00	65.00	110.00	
1890 S		2,808,000	50.00	55.00	65.00	110.00	
1891		6,329,476	50.00	60.00	70.00	125.00	
1891 M		2,749,592	50.00	55.00	65.00	110.00	
1891 S		2,596,000	50.00	55.00	65.00	110.00	
1892*		7,104,720	50.00	60.00	70.00	125.00	
1892 M		3,488,750	50.00	55.00	65.00	110.00	
1892 S		2,837,000	50.00	55.00	65.00	110.00	
1893 M		1,649,352	50.00	55.00	65.00	110.00	
1893 S		1,498,000	50.00	55.00	65.00	110.00	

*Counterfeits exist.

When L. C. Wyon died in 1891, he was succeeded by George William de Saulles, who was appointed Chief Engraver in 1893. De Saulles engraved the "veiled head" portrait from designs by Sir Thomas Brock.

Coins of this type were also minted at the Melbourne (M), Perth (P) and Sydney (S) mints. The mint mark appears on the ground line beneath the dragon. Proof coins of 1893 were issued in the specimen sets.

Diameter: 22.05mm; weight: 7.988 grams; composition: .917 gold, .083 copper; edge: reeded.

Date	Quantity Minted Proof	Quantity Minted Regular	Fine	V. F.	Ex. F.	Unc.	Proof
1893......(773)		6,898,260	$50.00	$55.00	$65.00	$100.00	$250.00
1893 M		1,914,400	50.00	55.00	65.00	100.00	
1893 S		1,346,000	47.50	50.00	60.00	90.00	
1894		3,782,611	47.50	50.00	60.00	85.00	
1894 M		4,166,874	47.50	50.00	60.00	85.00	
1894 S		3,067,000	47.50	50.00	60.00	85.00	
1895		2,285,317	47.50	50.00	60.00	85.00	
1895 M		4,165,869	47.50	50.00	60.00	85.00	
1895 S		2,758,000	47.50	50.00	60.00	85.00	
1896		3,334,065	47.50	50.00	60.00	85.00	
1896 M		4,456,932	47.50	50.00	60.00	85.00	
1896 S		2,544,000	50.00	55.00	65.00	100.00	
1897 M		5,130,565	47.50	50.00	60.00	85.00	
1897 S		2,532,000	47.50	50.00	60.00	85.00	
1898		4,361,347	47.50	50.00	60.00	85.00	
1898 M		5,509,138	47.50	50.00	60.00	85.00	
1898 S		2,548,000	50.00	55.00	65.00	100.00	
1899		7,515,978	47.50	50.00	60.00	85.00	
1899 M		5,579,157	47.50	50.00	60.00	85.00	
1899 P (Perth mint)		690,992	50.00	55.00	65.00	110.00	
1899 S		3,259,000	47.50	50.00	60.00	90.00	
1900		10,846,741	47.50	50.00	60.00	85.00	
1900 M		4,305,904	47.50	50.00	60.00	85.00	
1900 P		1,886,089	50.00	55.00	65.00	100.00	
1900 S		3,586,000	47.50	50.00	60.00	85.00	
1901		1,578,948	47.50	50.00	60.00	90.00	
1901 M		3,987,701	50.00	55.00	65.00	110.00	
1901 P		2,889,333	50.00	55.00	65.00	110.00	
1901 S		3,012,000	50.00	55.00	65.00	110.00	

Edward VII 1901-1910

The obverse portrait of King Edward was by de Saulles. The reverse continues to use the St. George design by Pistrucci. A branch of the Royal Mint was opened at Ottawa, Canada during this reign and sovereigns of this type

Gold Sovereigns

were coined at Canada (C), Melbourne (M), Perth (P) and Sydney (S). All of the branch mint coins have a mint mark on the ground beneath the dragon. The proof coins of 1902 have a dull matte finish.

Date	Quantity Minted Proof	Quantity Minted Regular	Fine	V. F.	Ex. F.	Unc.	Proof
1902....	(15,123)	4,737,796	$47.50	$50.00	$60.00	$75.00	$175.00
1902 M		4,267,157	50.00	55.00	65.00	90.00	
1902 P		4,289,122	50.00	55.00	65.00	90.00	
1902 S		2,813,000	50.00	55.00	65.00	90.00	
1903		8,888,627	47.50	50.00	60.00	70.00	
1903 M		3,521,780	47.50	50.00	60.00	75.00	
1903 P		4,674,783	47.50	50.00	60.00	75.00	
1903 S		2,806,000	47.50	50.00	60.00	75.00	
1904		10,041,369	47.50	50.00	60.00	70.00	
1904 M		3,743,897	47.50	50.00	60.00	75.00	
1904 P		4,506,756	47.50	50.00	60.00	75.00	
1904 S		2,986,000	50.00	55.00	65.00	90.00	
1905		5,910,403	47.50	50.00	60.00	85.00	
1905 M		3,633,838	47.50	50.00	60.00	75.00	
1905 P		4,876,193	47.50	50.00	60.00	75.00	
1905 S		2,778,000	47.50	50.00	60.00	75.00	
1906		10,466,981	47.50	50.00	60.00	70.00	
1906 M		3,657,853	47.50	50.00	60.00	75.00	
1906 P		4,829,817	47.50	50.00	60.00	75.00	
1906 S		2,792,000	47.50	50.00	60.00	75.00	
1907		18,458,663	47.50	50.00	60.00	70.00	
1907 M		3,332,691	47.50	50.00	60.00	75.00	
1907 P		4,972,289	47.50	50.00	60.00	75.00	
1907 S		2,539,000	47.50	50.00	60.00	75.00	
1908		11,729,006	47.50	50.00	60.00	70.00	
1908 C (Ottawa mint)		636	500.00	800.00	1,000	1,400	
1908 M		3,080,148	47.50	50.00	60.00	70.00	
1908 P		4,875,617	47.50	50.00	60.00	70.00	
1908 S		2,017,000	47.50	50.00	60.00	70.00	
1909		12,157,099	47.50	50.00	60.00	70.00	
1909 C		16,273	60.00	75.00	120.00	200.00	
1909 M		3,029,538	47.50	50.00	60.00	70.00	
1909 P		4,524,241	47.50	50.00	60.00	70.00	
1909 S		2,057,000	47.50	50.00	60.00	70.00	
1910		22,379,624	47.50	50.00	60.00	70.00	
1910 C		28,012	55.00	65.00	80.00	150.00	
1910 M		3,054,547	47.50	50.00	60.00	70.00	
1910 P		4,690,625	47.50	50.00	60.00	70.00	
1910 S		2,135,000	47.50	50.00	60.00	70.00	

George V 1910-1936

The portrait of George V was designed by Sir Bertram Mackennal and his initials B.M. are on the truncation of the King's neck. Although English sovereigns were struck each year from 1911 through 1917, it is doubtful if any gold was actually issued for circulation after 1915. Gold was needed for essentials purchased during the war and for this reason many of the gold coins in circulation were withdrawn. Those dated 1916 and 1917 were practically all exported and melted. Sovereigns were struck again in 1925, but these were solely for the Bank of England's gold reserves and were not intended for circulation.

The mintage shown for 1925 consists of 3,520,431 struck in 1925 (from badly worn gold coins held by the Bank of England), 138,000 in 1949, 318,000 in 1951 and 430,000 in 1952. The pieces coined in London in these latter years were from dies dated 1925. They were distributed by banks throughout the world to establish the sovereign as a current coin and thus prove that modern imitations struck privately in other countries were made in violation of counterfeiting laws.

Treasury notes ceased to be redeemable for gold in 1925.

Diameter: 22.05mm; weight: 7.988 grams; composition: .917 gold, .083 copper; edge: reeded.

Position of branch mint mark.

Date	Quantity Minted Proof	Quantity Minted Regular	Fine	V. F.	Ex. F.	Unc.	Proof
1911....	(3,764)	30,044,105	$47.50	$50.00	$55.00	$70.00	$400.00
1911 C		256,946	60.00	70.00	80.00	125.00	
1911 M		2,851,451	47.50	50.00	55.00	70.00	
1911 P		4,373,165	47.50	50.00	55.00	70.00	
1911 S		2,519,000	47.50	50.00	55.00	70.00	
1912		30,317,921	47.50	50.00	55.00	65.00	
1912 M		2,469,257	47.50	50.00	55.00	70.00	
1912 P		4,278,144	47.50	50.00	55.00	70.00	
1912 S		2,227,000	47.50	50.00	55.00	70.00	
1913		24,539,672	47.50	50.00	55.00	65.00	
1913 C		3,715	375.00	600.00	850.00	1,000	
1913 M		2,323,180	47.50	50.00	55.00	70.00	
1913 P		4,635,287	47.50	50.00	55.00	70.00	
1913 S		2,249,000	47.50	50.00	55.00	70.00	
1914		11,501,117	47.50	50.00	55.00	65.00	
1914 C		14,891	60.00	75.00	120.00	200.00	
1914 M		2,012,029	47.50	50.00	55.00	70.00	
1914 P		4,815,996	47.50	50.00	55.00	70.00	
1914 S		1,774,000	47.50	50.00	55.00	70.00	
1915		20,295,280	47.50	50.00	55.00	70.00	
1915 M		1,637,839	50.00	55.00	60.00	80.00	

Gold Sovereigns

Date	Quantity Minted	Fine	V. F.	Ex. F.	Unc.
1915 P	4,373,596	$50.00	$55.00	$60.00	$80.00
1915 S	1,346,000	50.00	55.00	60.00	80.00
1916	1,554,120	60.00	75.00	120.00	200.00
1916 C	6,111	——	——	——	——
1916 M	1,273,643	60.00	70.00	80.00	125.00
1916 P	4,096,771	50.00	55.00	65.00	90.00
1916 S	1,242,000	50.00	55.00	60.00	80.00
1917	1,014,714	——	——	——	——
1917 C	58,845	60.00	70.00	80.00	125.00
1917 M	934,469	50.00	55.00	60.00	80.00
1917 P	4,110,286	50.00	55.00	60.00	80.00
1917 S	1,666,000	50.00	55.00	60.00	75.00
1918 C	106,516	60.00	70.00	80.00	125.00
1918 I (Bombay mint)	1,295,372	47.50	50.00	55.00	70.00
1918 M	4,909,493	50.00	55.00	60.00	80.00
1918 P	3,812,884	47.50	50.00	55.00	70.00
1918 S	3,716,000	47.50	50.00	55.00	70.00
1919 C	135,889	60.00	70.00	80.00	125.00
1919 M	514,257	60.00	75.00	120.00	200.00
1919 P	2,995,216	50.00	55.00	60.00	80.00
1919 S	1,835,000	50.00	55.00	60.00	80.00
1920 M	530,266	100.00	200.00	350.00	600.00
1920 P	2,421,196	47.50	50.00	55.00	70.00
1920 S	360,000	150.00	300.00	400.00	——
1921 M	240,121				——
1921 P	2,134,360	50.00	55.00	65.00	90.00
1921 S	839,000			——	
1922 M	608,306				——
1922 P	2,298,884	47.50	50.00	55.00	70.00
1922 S	578,000	100.00	200.00	350.00	600.00
1923 M	510,870	75.00	150.00	300.00	500.00
1923 P	2,124,154	55.00	70.00	80.00	125.00
1923 S	416,000	200.00	400.00	500.00	
1923 SA (Pretoria mint)	719	(Proof)			600.00
1924 M	278,140	60.00	70.00	100.00	185.00
1924 P	1,464,416	60.00	70.00	90.00	175.00
1924 S	394,000			——	
1924 SA	3,184			——	
1925	4,406,431	50.00	55.00	60.00	75.00
1925 M	3,311,662	47.50	50.00	55.00	70.00
1925 P	1,837,901	60.00	75.00	120.00	200.00
1925 S	5,632,000	47.50	50.00	55.00	70.00
1925 SA	6,086,284	47.50	50.00	55.00	70.00
1926 M	211,107	60.00	75.00	90.00	150.00
1926 P	1,313,578	70.00	90.00	150.00	250.00
1926 S	1,031,050			——	
1926 SA	11,107,611	47.50	50.00	55.00	70.00
1927 M	310,156			——	
1927 P	1,383,544	60.00	75.00	125.00	200.00
1927 SA	16,379,704	47.50	50.00	55.00	70.00
1928 M	413,208	175.00	400.00	600.00	
1928 P	1,333,417	60.00	75.00	125.00	200.00
1928 SA	18,235,057	47.50	50.00	55.00	70.00

Gold Sovereigns

Only the Colonial coinage of George V sovereigns was continued after 1925. From 1929 through 1932 a modified and slightly smaller head is used on all issues.

Date	Proof	Quantity Minted Regular	Fine	V. F.	Ex. F.	Unc.	Proof
1929 M		436,719	$150.00	$300.00	$400.00	——	
1929 P		1,606,625	50.00	55.00	60.00	$80.00	
1929 SA		12,024,107	47.50	50.00	55.00	70.00	
1930 M		77,547	75.00	100.00	200.00	400.00	
1930 P		1,915,352	50.00	55.00	60.00	80.00	
1930 SA		10,027,756	47.50	50.00	55.00	70.00	
1931 M		57,779	90.00	125.00	250.00	475.00	
1931 P		1,173,568	47.50	50.00	55.00	75.00	
1931 SA		8,511,792	47.50	50.00	55.00	70.00	
1932 SA		1,066,680	50.00	55.00	60.00	80.00	

George VI 1936-1952

Sovereigns for George VI were minted only in 1937 and the entire issue was for proof or specimen sets. None was placed in circulation. The portrait is by Humphrey Paget, whose initials HP are placed below the truncation of the neck.

1937.....(5,501) Proof only.................................... $550.00

Elizabeth II 1952-

The portrait of Queen Elizabeth was designed by Mrs. Mary Gillick. The reverse is a continuation of the St. George design by Pistrucci.

A few specimen sets of gold coins were struck in 1953 and all are in official custody. The sovereigns struck in recent years were from stocks of worn gold held by the Bank of England and were coined to maintain the series and establish this as a current coin. Specimens were made available to the general public through banks. The sovereigns of 1958 and later have coarser edge reeding than the 1957 issue.

First Head 1957-1968 *Second Head 1974*

Gold Sovereigns

Date	Quantity Minted	Ex. F.	Unc.
1957	2,072,000	$55.00	$65.00
1958	8,700,140	50.00	60.00
1959	1,358,228	55.00	65.00
1962	3,000,000	50.00	60.00
1963	7,400,000	50.00	60.00
1964	3,000,000	50.00	60.00
1965	3,800,000	50.00	60.00
1966	7,050,000	50.00	60.00
1967	5,000,000	50.00	60.00
1968	4,203,000	50.00	60.00

In 1974 a new portrait was used for this coinage. The design was that by Arnold Machin first introduced on decimal coins.

1974	1,000,000	60.00	70.00

Counterfeit Gold Sovereigns

In recent years numerous counterfeit gold sovereigns have been struck in various parts of the world. Most of these are of Italian or Syrian origin, and frequently are made of full weight standard gold. They were made for use in world trade, where the British sovereign is usually valued higher than its bullion content.

Genuine British sovereigns dated 1925 and 1957 to date have been issued as bank coins to establish the fact that the sovereign is still a current coin and that the counterfeit pieces are illegal. In addition to this, the supply of genuine sovereigns has reduced the premium value placed on this coin and thus helped to eliminate the counterfeiting motive.

Most of the counterfeit sovereigns are found in mint condition, although some of them appear to be worn because of the poor relief caused by improper striking. They usually have a dull appearance and details are not as sharp as on genuine pieces. Some of them are very crude and have incomplete border beading. The edge reeding does not match regular coins in many cases.

Further points to look for in identifying counterfeit sovereigns include: date numerals of unequal size, blurred inscriptions, raised striations and dots, lack of details and below normal weight. Some appear to have been cast, although most are struck from false dies. In many instances dates are used that never occur on genuine coins. One counterfeit piece of George V is dated 1895 and another 1909 (S). Others from the South Africa Mint (SA) are dated prior to 1922 when the mint first opened.

Prevalent Counterfeit British Sovereigns

Victoria, Young head, London Mint — 1878, 1879
Victoria, Jubilee head, London Mint — 1887, 1889, 1891, 1892
Victoria, Veiled head, Melbourne Mint (M) — 1894, 1896
Edward VII, Perth Mint, Australia (P) — 1906
George V, London Mint — 1895, 1911 through 1920, 1923
George V, Canada Mint (C) — 1908, 1911, 1913
George V, India Mint (I) — 1918
George V, Melbourne Mint (M) — 1911, 1916
George V, Perth Mint, Australia (P) — 1913-1915, 1917-1919, 1921, 1922, 1929
George V, Sydney Mint, Australia (S) — 1909, 1917
George V, South Africa Mint (SA) — 1911-1913, 1917, 1920-1929, 1931
George V, Illegible mint mark — 1917, 1929

Enlarged details of counterfeit sovereign showing points of concern. Note especially the poor relief, dull appearance and incomplete areas. The numerous raised striations and dots are never found on genuine mint struck coins.

GOLD TWO POUNDS
George III 1760-1820

The idea of a two pound gold piece, or double sovereign, was first proposed late in the Regency under the reign of George III. The coin, however, never went beyond the pattern stage. Benedetto Pistrucci prepared these patterns, which show a laureate bust of the King on the obverse and the classic "St. George and the dragon" on the reverse.

Date	Quantity Minted	Fine	V. F.	Ex. F.	Unc.	Proof
1820	Pattern only			$5,000		$9,000

George IV 1820-1830

The St. George reverse by Pistrucci was used on the first coinage of George IV. J. B. Merlen, Assistant Mint Engraver, produced the obverse dies showing a large bare head of the King from a design by Sir Francis Chantrey. The engraver's initials JBM are below the bust.

Diameter: 28.40mm; weight: 15.976 grams; composition: .917 gold, .083 copper; edge: reeded.

Date		Fine	V. F.	Ex. F.	Unc.	Proof
1823		$350,00	$600.00	$750.00	$1,000	——

In 1825 a new type coinage was minted featuring a portrait of the King that was designed by Chantrey and engraved by W Wyon. The reverse shows a shield with the Royal Arms designed by Merlen. Coins of the second type were struck only as proofs and not intended for circulation.

Date	Quantity Minted Proof	Regular	Fine	V. F.	Ex. F.	Unc.	Proof
1825	Proof only						$2,250
1826	Proof only						2,000

William IV 1830-1837

Only proof or pattern pieces were struck in this series during the reign of William IV. The portrait was designed by Chantrey and engraved by Wyon. The square, crowned shield on the reverse was the work of J. B. Merlen.

1831	(225) Proof only						3,750

Victoria 1837-1901

No two pound pieces were issued during the reign of Queen Victoria until the Jubilee Head issue of 1887, when coins were struck for circulation and in proof for inclusion in the specimen sets. The bust was designed by Sir J. Boehm and engraved by Wyon. The reverse is a reinstatement of Pistrucci's St. George design. Dangerous counterfeits exist.

1887	(797)	91,345	$150.00	$200.00	$350.00	$500.00	$700.00

Gold Two Pounds

When G. W. de Saulle's "veiled head" of Victoria was adopted for coinage in 1893, a special issue of gold two pound pieces was minted. Proof specimens were included in the mint sets and a quantity of regular coins was issued for general circulation.

Date	Quantity Minted Proof	Quantity Minted Regular	Fine	V. Fine	Ex. Fine	Unc.	Proof
1893 . . . . . . (773)		52,212	$150.00	$200.00	$450.00	$600.00	$800.00

Edward VII 1901-1910

In accordance with custom, two pound pieces were issued during the first year of the reign of Edward VII in order to maintain the series. In addition to the pieces minted for circulation, proof coins were struck for the specimen sets. The proof coins all have a dull, matte finish and are quite unlike the brilliant proof coins issued in other years. The King's portrait was engraved by G. W. de Saulles, whose initials DES are beneath the bust.

| 1902 . . . . . (8,066) | | 45,807 | 150.00 | 200.00 | 350.00 | 500.00 | 700.00 |

Dangerous counterfeits exist.

George V 1910-1936

Gold two pound pieces for this reign were issued only in proof for the specimen sets and not for circulation. The portrait is by Sir Bertram Mackennal and the St. George design continued to be used on the reverse.

Date	Quantity Minted Proof	Regular		Proof
1911 ....(2,812)	Proof only			$900.00

Dangerous counterfeits exist.

George VI 1936-1952

The coronation sets of George VI contained a two pound gold piece identical in design to the other gold coins of this King. All of these were struck as proofs and none were placed in circulation. The portrait is by T. H. Paget.

1937 ....(5,501)	Proof only	650.00

Elizabeth II 1952-

A few specimens of a two pound gold piece were struck in 1953 to maintain the series. None was ever released, however, and all remain in official custody. The portrait is that designed by Mrs. Mary Gillick as used on the regular coinage of Queen Elizabeth. The reverse is the St. George design.

GOLD FIVE POUNDS

George III 1760-1820

Pattern five pound pieces were first struck in 1820, the last year of the Regency under the reign of George III. These are similar in appearance to the gold two pound pieces of this reign, which are also patterns. They are now extremely rare and seldom found in any collection.

Gold Five Pounds

George IV 1820-1830

A small number of proof five pound pieces were coined bearing the portrait of George IV designed by Chantrey and engraved by Merlen. These pieces were sold privately by the Mint Engraver, usually as part of a set in a special plush case. None was placed in circulation.

Date	Quantity Minted	Proof
1826	Proof only	$10,000

William IV 1830-1837

Patterns for the crown of William IV were struck in gold and because of their size have occasionally been included in collections in place of the five pound piece, which was never issued. The portrait was engraved by W. Wyon from a bust by Sir Francis Chantrey. Assistant Mint Engraver J. B. Merlen designed the shield used on the reverse. Because of their extreme rarity, these patterns are seldom seen outside of museums.

1831	Proof only	

Victoria 1837-1901

The first true issue of gold five pound coins took place on the occasion of the Queen's Golden Jubilee in 1887. Prior to that, William Wyon exhibited his outstanding skill as an engraver by preparing a pattern for this denomination in 1839. This truly classical design depicts the Queen as Una, standing beside a lion. The charming "young head" is similar to that used on the regular coinage. Dangerous counterfeits exist.

Date		Proof
1839 . . . . .Pattern		$13,000

The Jubilee coinage of Victoria has the usual design found on other coins of this series. The Queen's portrait was designed by Sir J. Boehm and Pistrucci's St. George design is used on the reverse. Proof specimens were struck for inclusion in the mint sets and a quantity was minted for general use. It is doubtful, however, if many ever saw actual circulation. Dangerous counterfeits exist.

Diameter: 36.02mm; weight: 39.94 grams; composition: .917 gold, .083 copper; edge: reeded.

Date	Quantity Minted Proof	Regular	Fine	V. F.	Ex. F.	Unc.	Proof
1887	(797)	53,844	$400.00	$600.00	$750.00	$1,000	$2,000

Gold five pound pieces were also issued at the time the "veiled head" design was first introduced in 1893. Proof coins were struck for the sets and others were made for circulation; few, however, were ever actually used as money. Dangerous counterfeits exist.

Gold Five Pounds

Date	Quantity Minted Proof	Regular	Fine	V. F.	Ex. F.	Unc.	Proof
1893 . . . . . . (773)		20,405	$600.00	$750.00	$1,000	$1,500	$3,000

Edward VII 1901-1910

King Edward's portrait was designed by G. W. de Saulles, whose initials DES are under the bust. In keeping with tradition, the St. George design continued in use, and a few coins of this denomination were struck to maintain the series and for inclusion in the specimen sets. The proof coins all have a dull, matte finish. Counterfeits exist.

Date	Proof	Regular	Fine	V. F.	Ex. F.	Unc.	Proof
1902 . . . . . (8,066)		34,911	600.00	750.00	1,000	1,250	1,500

George V 1910-1936

Proof specimens of the five pound coins were minted for George V, but only for inclusion in the coronation sets. The design is identical to other gold coins of this reign. Counterfeits exist.

Date	Quantity Minted Proof	Regular	Proof
1911 ....(2,812)	Proof only........................		$2,000

George VI 1936-1952

The coronation set of coins issued for George VI also included a gold five pound piece, in keeping with the sets of former years. Only the proof coins were struck, and none were issued for circulation. The portrait was designed by T. H. Paget.

1937 ....(5,501)	Proof only........................		1,500

Elizabeth II 1952-

A few specimens of this denomination were struck for the Queen's coronation, and to maintain the series. These coins were never released, and all remain in official custody. The design is identical to the two pound piece which was coined for the same purpose in 1953.

ENGLISH SPECIMEN SETS

In almost 150 years, only 13 official proof sets have been issued by Great Britain. Each set is unique in forming the only proof set of coins for its particular type. Not a great deal is known about the earlier sets, and therefore most "facts" concerning them are conjectural.

GEORGE IV 1826 ● The first specimen set offered for public sale. Contains farthing, halfpenny, penny, sixpence, shilling, half crown, crown, half sovereign, sovereign, two pounds gold and five pounds gold. Oval case is original. Very rare, probably less than 200 sets made. $15,000.

WILLIAM IV 1831 ● Contains farthing, halfpenny, penny, Maundy set, sixpence, shilling, half crown, crown, half sovereign, sovereign and two pounds gold. The gold five pounds was not included in the set. Round case is original. Occasionally seen with the extremely rare 1834 crown. Very rare set, less than 150 originally issued. $10,000.

VICTORIA 1839 ● Contains farthing, halfpenny, penny, Maundy set, groat, sixpence, shilling, half crown, crown, half sovereign, sovereign and five pounds gold "Una and the Lion." Considered by many the most desirable of all English specimen sets. The spade-shaped case is original. Intact complete sets are very rare. Approximately 300 were made. $16,000.

VICTORIA 1853 ● Contains the quarter-farthing, half-farthing, farthing, halfpenny, penny, Maundy set, groat, sixpence, shilling, florin, half crown, Gothic crown, half sovereign and sovereign. Seen in various shaped cases. Rarest of all English specimen sets; very few intact sets exist. $12,000.

VICTORIA 1887 ● Issued on her Golden Jubilee. Contains the threepence, sixpence, shilling, florin, half crown, double florin, crown, half sovereign, sovereign, two pounds and five pounds gold. 797 sets issued. Seen in a variety of cases, no single one of which is official. True proof sets are rare; selected uncirculated coins are sometimes unknowingly offered as proofs. $5,000. Short set, threepence to crown (seven pieces) 287 made. $700.00.

VICTORIA 1893 ● Contains the threepence, sixpence, shilling, florin, half crown, crown, half sovereign, sovereign, two pounds and five pounds gold. 773 sets made. Comes in various unofficial cases. Complete intact sets are rare. $6,000.   Short set (six silver pieces). $700.00.

EDWARD VII 1902 ● Issued by the Royal Mint in two forms: The "short" set containing all four Maundy coins, sixpence, shilling, florin, half crown, crown, half sovereign and sovereign, and the "long" set additionally containing the two pounds and five pounds gold. Original cases for both are of red leather. The surface of these coins is unlike any others in British numismatic history, having a matte finish. 8,066 long sets and 7,057 short sets issued. Long set. $2,750.   Short set. $700.00.

GEORGE V 1911 ● Issued by the Royal Mint in three forms: The silver set, containing 4 Maundy coins, sixpence, shilling, florin and half crown (2,241 sets made); the short set, including also the half sovereign and sovereign (952 sets made); and finally the long set, additionally containing the two pounds and five pounds gold (2,812 sets issued). Original cases are red leather; the silver set rarely seen in a cardboard box. About equal in rarity to 1887 and 1893 sets in actual availability. Silver set. $275.00. Short set. $900.00. Long set. $4,000.

GEORGE V 1927 ● Contains the threepence, sixpence, shilling, florin, half crown and crown. Very important set, as five of the six pieces are "proof only" issues. 15,030 sets made. Comes in both red cardboard and pale red leather cases. $300.00.

GEORGE VI 1937 ● Two separate sets issued in 1937: The gold set of half sovereign, sovereign, two pounds and five pounds (5,501 minted); and the minor set containing farthing, halfpenny, penny, brass threepence, Maundy set, sixpence, English reverse shilling, Scottish reverse shilling, florin, half crown and crown (26,402 sets struck). Both sets come separately in dark maroon leather cases. The minor set is infrequently seen in a red cardboard case. Gold set alone. $2,750. Minor set alone. $150.00.

GEORGE VI 1950 ● 17,513 sets issued for numismatic purposes. Contains the farthing, halfpenny, penny, threepence, sixpence, English shilling, Scottish shilling, florin and half crown. Issued in a red cardboard case. Heavy tarnish is normal. $80.00.

GEORGE VI 1951 ● Issued on the occasion of the Festival of Britain. Contains farthing, halfpenny, penny, threepence, sixpence, English shilling, Scottish shilling, florin, half crown and crown. 20,000 sets struck, most of which were hawked on the streets of London. Comes in a square pasteboard case (color maroon is commonest; blue is scarcest). $100.00.

ELIZABETH II 1953 ● Contains: farthing, halfpenny, penny, threepence, sixpence, English shilling, Scottish shilling, florin, half crown and crown. 40,000 sets issued. Original case is metal covered with dark maroon leatherette. A significant set, as 1953 was the only year coins of Elizabeth were struck bearing the words "BRITT: OMN" in the legend. $65.00.

ELIZABETH II 1970 ● Set contains eight coins, halfpenny to half crown. No coins of this date were issued for circulation. Packaged in a plastic case accompanied by a Royal Mint medallion. 750,000 sets were minted. $15.00.

ELIZABETH II 1971 ● Decimal coinage set. Contains six coins, half NP to fifty NP. Plastic case with mint medallion. $13.00.

INDEX

INDEX

BIBLIOGRAPHY

Allen, J. J. Cullimore — *Sovereigns of the British Empire,* London, 1965.

Becker, T. W. – *A Pageant of World Commemorative Coins,* Racine, 1962.

Bramah, E. — *English Regal Copper Coins,* London, 1929.

Brooke, G. C. — *English Coins,* third edition, London, 1950.

Duveen, Sir Geoffrey and H. G. Stride — *The History of the Gold Sovereign,* London, 1962.

Freeman, Michael J. — *The Bronze Coinage of Great Britain,* London, 1970.

Garside, H. — *British Imperial Copper and Bronze Coinage, 1920,* Supplement, 1925.

Haxby, J. A. and R. C. Willey — *Coins of Canada,* second edition, Racine, 1972.

Henfrey, Henry W. — *A Guide to the Study of English Coins,* London, 1885.

Interpol — *Counterfeits and Forgeries,* Paris, 1961.

Josset, C. R. — *Money In Great Britain and Ireland,* Rutland, Vt., 1971.

Leming, Joseph — *From Barter to Banking,* New York, 1940.

Montagu, H. — *The Copper, Tin and Bronze Coinage of England,* London, 1893.

Peck, C. Wilson — *English Copper, Tin and Bronze Coins in the British Museum 1558-1958,* London, 1964.

Rayner, P. Alan — *The Designers and Engravers of the English Milled Coinage, 1662 to 1953,* London, 1954.

Royal Mint — *Annual Report of the Royal Mint,* Various dates, London.

Seaby, H. A. — *Coins of England and the United Kingdom,* Parts 1 and 2, 14th Edition, London, 1975.

Seaby, H. A. and P. A. Rayner — *The English Silver Coinage From 1649,* London, 1974.

Seaby, H. A. — *Standard Catalogue of British Coins,* Part II, London, 1974.

Seaby, Peter — *The Story of the English Coinage,* London, 1952.

Seaby, P. J. and Monica Bussell — *British Copper Coins and Their Values,* London, 1969.

Spink & Son, Ltd. — *The Milled Silver Coinage of England,* London, 1925.

Spink & Son, Ltd. — *The Milled Coinage of England, 1662-1946,* London, 1950 with supplement 1958.

Thorburn, Col. W. Stewart — *A Guide to the Coins of Great Britain and Ireland,* second edition, London, 1886.

Trowbridge, Richard J. — *Maundy Coins of Great Britain,* Glendale, Cal., 1972.

Yeoman, R. S. — *A Catalog of Modern World Coins,* eleventh edition, Racine, 1974.

Yeoman, R. S. — *Current Coins of the World,* sixth edition, Racine, 1974.